SPIRITUAL WARFARE:

SPIRITUAL WARFARE:

A HOW TO GUIDE FOR DEFEATING SATAN

PUTTING ON THE ARMOR OF GOD

WITH REV. SANDRA H. HATCHELL, PH.D.

TATE PUBLISHING & *Enterprises*

Tate Publishing is committed to excellence in the publishing industry. Our staff of highly trained professionals, including editors, graphic designers, and marketing personnel, work together to produce the very finest books available. The company reflects the philosophy established by the founders, based on Psalms 68:11,

"The Lord Gave The Word And Great Was The Company Of Those Who Published It."

If you would like further information, please contact us:
1.888.361.9473 | www.tatepublishing.com
Tate Publishing & Enterprises, llc | 127 E. Trade Center Terrace
Mustang, Oklahoma 73064 USA

Defeating Satan: A How to Guide to Spiritual Warfare

Scripture quotations marked "NIV" are taken from the Holy Bible, New International Version ®, Copyright © 1973, 1978, 1984 by International Bible Society. Used by permission of Zondervan Publishing House. All rights reserved.

The opinions expressed by the author are not necessarily those of Tate Publishing, LLC.

This book is designed to provide accurate and authoritative information with regard to the subject matter covered. This information is given with the understanding that neither the author nor Tate Publishing, LLC is engaged in rendering legal, professional advice. Since the details of your situation are fact dependent, you should additionally seek the services of a competent professional.

Book design copyright © 2007 by Tate Publishing, LLC. All rights reserved.
Cover design by Elizabeth Mason
Interior design by Chris Webb

Published in the United States of America

ISBN: 978-1-5988664-3-8
07.02.06

Acknowledgments

To my husband Ralph, who was patient during all the hours I spent "chained" to the research books and the computer. To my daughter Alex, who worked through the study with me to ask questions and suggest clarifications. Her questions were invaluable in assisting me to keep it simple and usable for everyone. She also gave hours in editing the scripture to make sure that I had copied them correctly. My sincere thanks to Betty R. Rhode who edited for grammar and structural flow. To Carolyne Rogerson who supported me and encouraged me during the two years of this process. There are so many others that encouraged, questioned, and prayed for me during the writing of this book. My prayer partners, who keep me constantly covered in prayer that Satan had no power to block the research and writing of this body of work. Lastly, to the person who triggered the work from the start. Her belief that there was no truth in me, and no hope for my redemption as a person or as a pastor created a crisis of life and of faith that sent me on this journey. I will always be grateful.

TABLE OF CONTENTS

Preface

From the beginning of time there have been stories of Lucifer, a great angel who challenged the rule of God, because of his arrogance and pride and was cast out of Heaven. From that time to the present, according to the scriptures, Lucifer and his fallen angels have worked their evil will to spreading mayhem, fear, death, and destruction throughout the world.

Why does God allow Satan and demons to exist? To ask this question another way, why didn't God send Satan and the angels who followed him in his rebellion against God to the lake of fire immediately after they sinned? We could ask a similar question with regard to the human race. Why didn't God wipe out Adam and Eve when they sinned? Why doesn't God bring us sudden death when we sin? The only answer to such questions is that His grace withstands His judgment.

When God chose to allow evil to come into the world, He chose the best possible plan to bring the most possible glory to Himself. God uses what He allows the devil and his demons to do to teach us the grace we need for maturity in Christ. When we cling to Him, He sees us through the toughest battles Satan can wage. We can triumph in Christ. (Lightner, *Angels, Satan, and Demons*, pg. 172)

In order to live in this world with them and their evil presence and influence means we must know them. To live in safety and against invisible evil we must have all the warning and protection Christ can give us, we must be forewarned and forearmed. (Masello, *Fallen Angels*, pg.11)

The devil (and doubtless his demons) tempt God's people to

sin. But there is no teaching in the Bible that the devil and demons cause people to sin. James wrote that the cause of our sin is not God, for He does not tempt anyone to evil (James1:13). What then is the source of temptation and eventual sin? "But each one is tempted when he is carried away and enticed by his own lust. Then when lust has conceived, it gives birth to sin; and when sin is accomplished, it brings forth death" (James 1:14–15). The devil and demons do not make us do anything, and that includes sin. We choose to sin just as surely as we choose not to sin. (Lightner, *Angels, Satan, and Demons*, pg. 173)

———————

As a pastor, I have wondered how to help my congregations and myself deal with the idea of evil, Satan, and sin. I began this research because my personal world seems to be falling apart. My husband was about to have serious surgery, my daughter was extremely ill, my friends were angry at me, my church was struggling, and I felt lost and alone. A friend asked me, was this turmoil due to Satan? On the other hand, was it just a fluke that I would have to survive? Therefore, I began to research and delve into Satan's activities and methods. This Bible study is the result of that research. The devil has so many ways to move and function among us. These ways are individual and personal. What constitutes temptation for me will have little appeal for someone else. Therefore, this study is a general lens through which we can focus on Satan, his ways, power, and our victory over him through Jesus Christ our Lord.

The Bible is clear that Christians are the objects of Satan's and his demon's attacks. We are not told, however, how we are to distinguish between their opposition and the conflicts and difficulties we bring on ourselves. In other words, there are times when we are reaping the results of poor or bad decisions and Satan and his demons may not be involved.

It is best, therefore, for us to evaluate our own behavior before blaming Satan and demons for every obstacle and problem we face. When we discover that we ourselves are the cause of the problem, we should take definite steps not to repeat past mistakes or sins. If God's Spirit convinces us we are being assaulted by Satan and demons, we need to remind ourselves of the armor of Ephesians 6, which God has provided for us. In the strength of God's Spirit we then can resist Satan and claim victory in Christ. (Lightner, *Angels, Satan, and Demons*, pg. 173)

Introduction to Bible study

As you go through this Bible study, remember that Satan cannot read your thoughts. As you go to God in prayer, for repentance, for guidance, and for putting on the armor of God, pray out loud. As you go through the inventory of needs, praise and the prayers remember these are critical issues between you and God, but He is with you. (Rogerson, *Angels Bible Study*)

This Bible study is a comprehensive process of submitting to God and resisting the devil. It doesn't matter if there are evil spirits present; the real issue is our relationship with God. Remember, thoughts and self-talk have no power over us unless we believe them and act upon them. There will be times and places in this study that you might meet with resistance or opposition in your mind and heart, these are the times when we need to stop and pray. Throughout this study we will be asking God to lead us in our own needs and repentance and areas that we need to be led to knowledge of truth which will set us free. This will be different for each of us. Be open to the leading of the Holy Spirit, trusting in what you hear through his leading.

Below is a prayer that will assist us in beginning the inventory.

Dear heavenly Father, I ask You to bring to my mind anything and everything that I have done knowingly or unknowingly that interferes with my relationship with You, with others and with me. As I answer these questions guide me in truth. Give me strength to be honest with You and with myself, that I might trust in the healing of my spirit and increase my faith and strengthen my walk

and testimony for Christ. In Jesus' name I pray. Amen
(Anderson, The Bondage Breaker, pg. 189)

Answer each question as honestly as possible. No one will see
your inventory except you and God. List everything under each
section even if it was in fun or just a game. Remember, Satan
will try to take advantage of anything he can in our lives, so be
as thorough as possible. If something comes to mind and you're
not sure what to do about it, or where to put it, trust the Spirit of
God as He leads and guides you. If there is something that comes
to mind and there is no section for it to be listed, feel free to add
it because God gave it to you to look at. (Anderson, *The Steps to
Freedom in Christ*, pg 2)

Confidential Personal Inventory

I. Personal Information

Name
Telephone
Address
Age
Church Affiliation
Schools attended
Highest grade completed; degrees earned
Marital status
Previous marriage/divorce
Number of Children
Any Miscarriages
Any abortions
Vocation

Present

Past

Have you ever been arrested?

Family History

A. Religious

1. To your knowledge, have any of your parents, aunts, uncles, grandparents, great-grandparents, or any other family members that you might know about, ever been involved in any occult, cultic, or non-Christian religious practices?

Briefly explain your parents' Christian experience (that is, were they Christians, and did they profess and live their Christianity?)

1. Did you and your siblings grow up in a faith community? What kind?

2. Did you at some point quit? Why and when did you return to a faith community and why?

3. Briefly write out your faith journey.

B. Marital Status

1. Are your parents presently married or divorced? Explain

2. Do you have any step or half siblings?

3. Describe the relationship between step parents, siblings or half siblings.

4. Was there a sense of security and harmony in your home during the first twelve years of your life?

5. Was your father clearly the head of the home, or was there a role reversal in which your mother ruled the home? Explain.

6. How did your father treat your mother?

7. To your knowledge, were any of your parents or grandparents ever involved in an adulterous affair?

C. Health

1. Are there any addictive problems in your family (alcohol, drugs, and so on)?

2. Is there any history of mental illness?

3. Is there any history of the following ailments in your family? (Please circle.)
   Tuberculosis (TB)   heart disease   diabetes   cancer
   Ulcers   glandular problems   other

4. How would you describe your families concern for:
   a. diet
   b. exercise
   c. rest

5. Is there or was there a family secret? How was that secret maintained? Is it still being maintained and by whom?

D. Family relationships

1. Were your parents strict or permissive?

2. Were there favored children?

3. Describe your placement in the family, i.e. first child, second child, third etc.

4. Describe how any favored status affected you and how you felt and feel about that status and roles each of the children might have had.

E. Where do your parents or grandparents originate from? How and why they got here?

1. At what age did your parents leave home? Why

2. At what age did you leave home? Why

3. List brothers and sisters. List similarities between you and your siblings and your parents and their siblings.

4. Are you adopted?

History of Personal Health

A. Physical

1. Describe your eating habit (that is; junk food addict,

eat regular or sporadically, balanced diet, and so on).

2. Do you have any addictions or cravings that you find difficult to control (sweets, drugs, alcohol, food in general, other)?

3. Are you presently under any kind of medication for either physical or psychological reasons?

4. Do you have any problem sleeping? Are you having recurring nightmares or disturbances?

5. Does your present schedule allow for regular periods of rest and relaxation?

6. Have you ever been physically beaten, sexually molested or lived with verbal abuse? Explain

7. How is your exercise routine? When and how much?

8. What do you do for relaxation?

9. How are you spiritually renewed?

10. Is there a place that you go that gives you peace, that you feel safe and renewed?

B. Mental

1. How much time do you spend in any of the following categories? List each item and approximate time. Worry; negative thinking; daydreaming; lustful thoughts; obsessive thoughts; thoughts of inferiority; insecurity; thoughts of inadequacy; doubts; jealousy, regrets?

2. Do you spend much time wishing you were somebody else or fantasizing that you were a different person? Do you imagine yourself living at a different time, a different place, or under different circumstances? Explain

3. How many hours of TV do you watch per week? List your five favorite programs.

4. How many hours do you spend each week reading? What do you read primarily (newspaper, magazines, books, other)?

5. Would you consider yourself to be an optimist or a pessimist (that is, do you have a tendency to see the good in people and life or the bad)?

6. Have you ever thought that maybe you were "Cracking up"? Do you presently feat that possibility? Explain

7. Do you have regular devotions in the Bible? Where and when, and to what extent?

8. Do you find prayer difficult mentally? Explain

9. When attending church or other Christian ministries, are you plagued by foul thoughts, jealousies, or other mental harassment? Explain

10. Do you listen to music a lot? What type do you enjoy?

11. Are you an introvert or extravert spiritually? (An introvert is fed within themselves and extravert is fed outside themselves. Do you talk out your problems, fears and doubts with someone else or do you hold them within yourself until you have thought

through the situation completely before you share it with others?)

C. Emotional

1. Which of the following emotions do you struggle with? This is defined as an ongoing struggle not the day to day situations of life. (Please circle)
    Frustration   fear of death   anger
    Fear of losing your mind   anxiety   depression
    Fear of being hurt   fear of man   bitterness
    Fear of failure   hatred   worthlessness
    Fear of Satan

2. Which of the above listed emotions do you feel are sinful? Why?

3. Concerning your emotions, whether positive or negative, which of the following best describes you? Readily express my emotions, express some of my emotions, but not all, readily acknowledge their presence, but am reserved in expressing them, tend to suppress my emotions, find it safest not to express how I feel, tend to disregard how I feel since I cannot trust my feelings, consciously or sub-consciously deny them; it's too painful to deal with them, express some of my emotions, but not all, or hide them under the guise of other emotions.

4. Do you presently know someone with whom you could be emotionally honest (that is, you could tell this person exactly how feel about yourself, life, and other people)?

5. How important is it that we are emotionally honest before God? Do you feel that you are?

6. What are your greatest fears or phobias? How do they interfere with or disrupt your life?

7. What gives you joy, fulfillment, satisfaction, and contentment?

8. What are your goals, hopes, and dreams? For yourself, your children.

9. Do you have a mentor?

D. Spiritual History

1. If you were to die tonight, do you know where you would spend eternity?

2. Suppose you die tonight and appear before God

in heaven, and He asks you, "By what right should I allow you into My presence?" How would you answer Him?

3. (John 5:11–12) says, "God has given us eternal life, and this life is in His Son. He who has the Son has the life; he who does not have the Son of God does not have the life."
   a. Do you believe the statement above?

   b. When did you receive Him (John 1:12)?

   c. How do you know that you received Him?

4. Are you plagued by doubts about your salvation?

5. Are you presently enjoying fellowship with other believers, and if so, where and when?

6. Are you under the authority of a local church where the Bible is taught? Do you regularly support it with your time, talent, and treasure? If not, why not?

7. Describe what you get from worship.

8. What parts of a worship service do you feel you receive the most spiritual feeding?

E. General

1. Do you presently have any grudges? List against who, what, and why.

2. Do you have any areas or issues that make you inflexible or unreasonable?

3. Are you compulsive, obsessive, or do you have pet peeves? How do these manifest themselves?

4. Do you feel there are attitudes or actions that you need to grow in or out of?

5. List the people you have hurt and need forgiveness from.

6. List the people who have hurt you, and how they hurt you. Whether you think they might have been aware they hurt you or unaware.

7. What do you think are the areas of your life that bother or cause others to stumble?

8. Do you have any prejudices? People places or things, list them.

9. Do you have any addictions or habits that you feel are detrimental to yourself, others or your witness?

10. Are there areas that you are deceptive to yourself, such as, believing that acquiring money and things will bring lasting happiness, believing that consuming food and alcohol excessively will make me happy, believing that a great body and personality will get me what I want, believing that gratifying sexual lust will bring lasting satisfaction, believing that I can sin and get away with it and not have it affect my heart, believing that I need more than what God has given me in Christ, believing that I can do whatever I want and no one can touch me, believing that unrighteous people who refuse to accept Christ go to heaven anyway, believing that I can hang around bad company and not become corrupted, believing that there are no consequences on earth for my sin, believing that I must gain the approval of certain people in order to be happy, believing that I must measure up to certain standards in order to feel good about myself.

11. How do you defend yourself? Here are some possibilities: deny reality, fantasizing, which includes escaping reality through daydreaming, TV, movies, music, computer, drugs, alcohol, food; emotional isolation, which can be defined as keeping people at a distance to avoid rejection; regression, which is reverting back to a less threatening time; displaced anger, projection, rationalization or making excuses, etc.

12. Are there places in your life that you need to forgive yourself for?

13. Have you ever been angry with God or afraid to be angry with God?

14. What are the consistent lies you tell yourself?

15. What areas and issues in your life do you tend to "handle myself" and issues you give to God, but then continue to try to fix yourself?

16. Are there issues in your life that make you feel trapped?

17. Do you have habits that you can't seem to break?

18. Areas you have given up believing God can fix (more to the point, God can but we can't seem to allow?)

19. Do you believe you can be forgiven, by God, others or yourself, if not explain reason, action, feeling or thought. What leads you to this belief?

20. Have you ever participated in any of the following? Ouija board; spells or curses, automatic writing, trances, spirit guides, fortune telling, tarot cards, witchcraft, sorcery, palm reading, Satanism, séances, black or white magic, Dungeons & Dragons and similar games, blood pacts, cutting yourself on purpose, superstitions, crystals, Christian Science or the Church of Scientology, The Unification Church. List these on your sheet and write any explanation that you feel you may need to be able to move through the issues toward repentance and healing. Look at motivations or issues that drew you to actions such as these. These are not always negative, but places where you can see God's grace at work in your life. (That grace which God gives that can be the beginning of the process of leading you to Him.)

21. Have you ever seen, heard, or felt a spiritual being in your room or presence?

22. Do you have recurring nightmares?

23. Have you ever had an imaginary friend, or a spirit guide offering you guidance and companionship?

24. Have you ever heard voices in your head or had repeating, nagging thoughts such as I'm dumb, I'm ugly, nobody loves me. As if there were a conversation going on inside your head?

25. Have you ever consulted a medium or spiritist?

26. Have you ever made a secret vow or pact?

27. Have you ever been involved in a satanic ritual of any kind, or attended a concert in which Satan was the focus?

28. What other spiritual experiences have you had that were evil, confusing or frightening?

29. Listed below are areas where people or things have become more important to us than the true God, Jesus Christ. Most of these areas are not evil; they only become evil when we focus on them rather

than on Christ and his power to overcome them. Check each item that at times you have or can become obsessive in. Explain if possible the emotion or "nurtured" feeling that the focus on this activity or person gives you. Ambition, food or any substance, money, possessions, computer games, financial security, rock stars, celebrities, athletes, church activities, physical fitness, fun/pleasure, ministry, appearance/image, work, business/activities, friends, power, control, boyfriend or girlfriend, popularity or the opinion of others, spouse, knowledge, being right, children, parents, and hobbies.

F. SEEKING FORGIVENESS AND FORGIVING OTHERS

The Process of Seeking Forgiveness

1. Write out what you did wrong and why you did it.

2. How did you feel when you were writing the answer to above question?

3. How did you react from those feelings?

4. Think through exactly how you will ask them to forgive you. Be sure to:
    a. Label your action as "wrong."
    b. Be specific and admit what you did.
    c. Make no defenses or excuses.
    d. Do not blame the other people, and do not expect or demand that they ask for your forgiveness.
    e. Your confession should lead to the direct question: "Will you forgive me?"

5. Make sure you have already forgiven them for whatever they may have done to you.

6. Seek the right place and the right time to approach the offended person.

7. Ask for forgiveness in person with anyone with whom you can talk face-to-face with the following exception: *Do not go alone* when your safety is in danger.

8. *Do not write a letter* except where no other means of communication is possible. A letter can be very easily misread or misunderstood; a letter can be read by the wrong people (those having nothing to do with

the offense or the confession); a letter can be kept when it should have been destroyed.

9. Once you sincerely seek forgiveness, you are free, whether the other person forgives you or not (Romans 12:18).

10. After forgiveness, fellowship with God in worship (Matthew 5:24).

The Process of Offering Forgiveness

1. Write out what you feel they did to you, pray over it and burn it.

2. How did you feel?

3. How did you react; anger, betrayal, etc.

4. How you continue to inflict damage to yourself due to the situation?

5. Do you believe there is anything you can do about correcting the relationship?

6. Do you believe there is anything that you did that assisted in creating the problem?

7. Pray for forgiveness within yourself that you might also look at forgiving them.

8. If it is possible to talk with that person, pray and then talk.

After completing the inventory and carefully evaluating yourself, you will have a clearer idea of how Satan has been an influence in your life. As you work through the bible study you will begin to feel a freedom and strength as you begin to heal.

Parts of the process of seeking and offering forgiveness was taken from Neil Anderson's book, *The Steps to Freedom in Christ*, pg. 2

The Origin of Satan and Rebellion of Lucifer

The Word of God needs to be systematically read and studied as it relates to our enemies. Biblical insight into how Satan operates, where he comes from, and who he is, provides strong equipment in spiritual warfare. The believers, intent on claiming all of their victories in the Lord Jesus Christ, should familiarize themselves with basic biblical information about our enemy.

> *The word of the Lord came to me: "Son of man, say to the ruler of Tyre, 'this is what the Sovereign Lord says: "In the pride of your heart you say, 'I am a god; I sit on the throne of a god in the heart of the seas."' But you are a man and not a god, though you think you are as wise as a god. "You will die the death of the uncircumcised at the hands of foreigners. I have spoken, declares the Sovereign LORD."' The word of the LORD came to me: "Son of man, take up a lament concerning the king of Tyre and say to him: 'This is what the Sovereign LORD says: "'You were the model of perfection, full of wisdom and perfect in beauty. You were in Eden, the garden of God; every precious stone adorned you: ruby, topaz and emerald, chrysolite, onyx, and jasper, sapphire, turquoise and beryl. Your settings and mountings were made of gold; on the day you were created they were prepared. You were anointed as a guardian cherub, for so I ordained you. You were on the holy mount of God; you walked among*

the fiery stones. You were blameless in your ways from the day you were created till wickedness was found in you. Through your widespread trade you were filled with violence, and you sinned. So I drove you in disgrace from the mount of God, and I expelled you, O guardian cherub, from among the fiery stones. Your heart became proud on account of your beauty, and you corrupted your wisdom because of your splendor. So I threw you to the earth; I made a spectacle of you before kings. By your many sins and dishonest trade you have desecrated your sanctuaries. So I made a fire come out from you, and it consumed you, and I reduced you to ashes on the ground in the sight of all who were watching. Ezekiel 28:1-2, 10-18*

Ezekiel prophesied in the sixth century b.c. He grew up in Jerusalem and lived there until he, along with many other Jews, was taken captive by Nebuchadnezzar to Babylon. There he had relative freedom and prophesied over a period of twenty-two years. Ezekiel's primary ministry was to the Jewish exiles in Babylonia.

God called Ezekiel to keep before the exiles the sins that cause them to be there. Along with that he also encouraged them by reminding them of God's faithfulness to the promises He made to them in His covenants. The first twenty four chapters of the Book of Ezekiel were written before Jerusalem fell to the Babylonians.

In the section on the coming judgment on Gentile nations, Ezekiel predicted the fall of "the leader of Tyre." There is little doubt that this verse refers to the historic figure Ethbaal III, who was at the time the ruler over the Phoenician seacoast city of Tyre. He was a very proud man, boastful of his many achievements. Ezekiel denounced him for his sinful pride and predicted his coming destruction and disgrace. But behind the human leader is Satan the superhuman leader.

Interestingly, in verse 12, Ezekiel introduced one whom he called "the king of Tyre." This king is not the same person as "the leader of Tyre" in verse 2, because for one thing, Ezekiel made some unusual statements about this "king": "You had the seal of perfection"; you were "full of wisdom and perfect in beauty"; "You were in Eden, the garden of God"; "You were blameless."

The person in verse 2 is called a man, but the one is verses 11–18 is "the anointed cherub" and the "Covering cherub." Also, twice Ezekiel said this one was "created." The superlative language in "perfect" and "blameless" fits Satan in his pre-fallen state far better than it does any human leader.

Before his fall Satan had great privileges. He was indeed the greatest of all God's creatures. The cherubim are a special class of angelic beings, who serve as guardians of God's holiness (Genesis 3:24).

In his vision of God, Ezekiel saw "four living beings" (Ezekiel 1:5), whom he later identified as cherubim. If this cherub in 28:14 is a description of Satan before his fall, it would mean he served, along with other angels, as a protector or honor guard of God's presence and holiness.

This cherub Ezekiel called "the king of Tyre" was at one time "in Eden, the garden of God." "The holy mountain of God" seems to refer to the very presence of God from which Satan was "cast." This casting out represents God's judgment on Satan because of his sin: "unrighteousness was found in you," "you were internally filled with violence," "you sinned," "your heart was lifted up because of your beauty," "you corrupted your wisdom by reason of your splendor," "the multitude of you iniquities," your "unrighteousness." At the time of his sin he was barred from his former position in God's government, though he still has access to God to accuse His people. (Lightner, *Angels, Satan, and Demons*, pgs. 68–70)

The historical fact of this verse is that there are consequences for sin. Satan is created full of wisdom and beauty. He was given a place on God's holy mountain. He was created a holy and righteous being. Because of pride, Satan was banished from heaven and from the presence of God.

> *How you have fallen from heaven, O morning star, son of the dawn! You have been cast down to the earth, you who once laid low the nations! You said in your heart I will ascend to the heaven; I will raise my throne above stars of God; I will sit enthroned on the mount of assembly on the utmost heights of the sacred mountain; I will ascend above the tops of the clouds; I will make myself like the most high.* **Isaiah 14: 12–14**

Isaiah 14 begins with a taunt of the King of Babylon but turns to the evil that is behind the king, Satan. Satan wants five things. They are shown in the five "I wills" of the passage: Ascend to the heaven, raise my throne above the stars of God, sit enthroned on the mount of the assembly, ascend above the tops of the clouds and make myself like the most high. "Stars of God" refers to the holy angels of God. Satan wanted to rule over the angels of God, yet not answer to God. "Mount of assembly" refers to the center of God's kingdom rule. This expression belongs only to God. It speaks about absolute control. Satan wants to control all the affairs of the universe. In the Bible, clouds often represent the Glory of God. There are 100 references where clouds relate to the Presence and Glory of God. Satan is saying here that he is going to rise higher than the Glory of God. Satan wanted to be above God. He wanted no competition. He wanted the privilege of God, so he declared his independence.

How did Satan come to be referred to as "son of the morning"? In part, it was because his name, Lucifer, was the name the Romans had given to the morning star, the last star each day to be obscured by the rising sun, (and partly it was because) in one ancient myth, of Hebrew origin, this same morning star had tried to out-blaze the sun itself, but had, of course, been vanquished in the end. The close analogy to Lucifer, the bright angel who had in his pride thought to displace God Himself and was brought down because of it, isn't hard to see (Masello, *Fallen Angels*, pg. 20).

No one knows for certain when Satan committed this awful sin of arrogance, which sealed his eternal doom. We do know he and other angels sinned before our first parents sinned, because Satan was there using the serpent in the garden to tempt them to sin. (Zeller, *The Fall of Satan, When Did This Take Place?*, photocopy) When Satan sinned, he was "fallen from heaven" and "cut down to the earth." The "star of the morning, the son of the dawn," became Satan the deceiver. He "weakened the nations," "made the earth tremble," "shook kingdoms," and "made the world like a wilderness." In the future Satan will be "thrust down to Sheol," and ultimately his eternal destiny will be in the lake of fire. (Lightner, *Angels, Satan, and Demons*, pg. 73)

For clarifications consider Isaiah 2:2 and Psalm 48:1–2

*In the last days the **mountain of the LORD's temple** will be established as chief among the mountains; it will be raised above the hills, and all nations will stream to it.* **Isaiah 2:2**

*Great is the LORD, and most worthy of praise, is **the city of our God, his holy mountain**. It is beautiful in its loftiness, the joy of the whole earth. Like the utmost heights of Zaphon is Mount Zion, the city of the Great King.* **Psalm 48:1–2**

Zaphon refers to a sacred mountain or the direction North (Jeremiah, Angels the Host of Heaven, pg. 60–61). The mountain of assembly may refer to Zion, sometimes called the mountain of God. This then would point to Satan's desire to rule as sovereign in place of God. (Lightner, Angels, Satan, and Demons, pg. 72)

Is Satan Real?

The Bible is full of references to Satan. He is also called by a large number of other names. He is referred to in seven books of the Old Testament. Every writer of the New Testament wrote of him. In the Gospels, Satan is mentioned twenty-nine times, and in twenty-five of these Christ was speaking. Early in the Bible and in human history Satan appeared, and he did so without explanation.

We must acknowledge that God, as we have seen earlier, created all the angels. And since He is God, He created them holy and sinless. The angels must be included in God's assessment of His creative work of creation, when He said, "It is very good" (Genesis 1:31). This is true of angels, whether they were created before or after, God created the people and things mentioned in Genesis.

Contrary to the thinking of some, Satan and the devil are not merely names for evil powers and bad things that happen in the world. Satan is just as much a person as God is. Personal pronouns are used of Satan throughout the Bible. The devil is often presented, and his evil plans described in association with other persons. (Lightner, *Angels, Satan, and Demons*, pg. 66)

No doctrine inside the precincts of the Christian Church is received with greater reserve and hesitation, even to the point of outright denial, than the doctrine of original sin . . . the doctrine of original sin is met with either embarrassed silence, outright denial, or at a minimum a kind of half hearted lip service that does not exactly deny the doctrine but has no idea how to place it inside the devout life (Oakes, *Original Sin: A disputation*, pg. 16).

In this doctrine of Original sin, Satan achieved his desire. His *power to tempt* Eve proves insurmountable. Despite all God's precautions, and there were many, the creatures He loved so dearly rebel against His rule.

Christianity is stuck with the devil, whether we like it or not. Any Christian group or denomination should not be taken seriously if they do not take the devil seriously. One of the things the devil wants is for Christians to deny his existence. If believing in the existence of the devil offends, if it is a stumbling block, then everything else about Christianity should be offensive.

The Fourth Lateran Council of 1215 a.d. taught: "The devil and the other demons were indeed created naturally good by God, but they became evil of their own doing." (*The Catechism of the Catholic Church*, Part One 98, no. 268).

If we decide against the existence of the devil, we are essentially deciding against the integrity of the Christian faith. If we take out all the verses that reference the devil, demons, principalities, powers, evil spirits, the evil one, unclean spirits, fallen angels, the antichrist, the beast, and the dragon, we would do extreme violence to the primary source of our faith.

Satan, this fearful being, apparently created as one of the Cherubim and anointed for a position of great authority, perhaps over the primitive creation that was "formless and void," fell through pride. His "I Wills" mark the introduction of sin into the universe. Cast out of heaven, he makes earth and air the scene of his tireless activity. After the creation of man he entered into the serpent and, beguiling Eve by his subtlety, secured the downfall of Adam and through him the race, and the entrance of sin into the world of man.

Since Satan is not omnipresent, that is, everywhere present at the same time, the only way to account for all the opposition to God, deceit, and waywardness of God's people is to acknowledge that Satan's angels are assisting him. (Lightner, *Angels, Satan, and Demons*, pg. 87)

The Adamic covenant promised the ultimate defeat of Satan through the "seed" of woman. It was at that time Satan began his warfare against the work of God, which still continues to this day. The present world system, organized upon the principles of force, greed, selfishness, ambition, and sinful pleasure, is his work and was the bribe which Satan offered to Christ. Of that world system he is prince, and god. As "prince of power of the air" he is at the head of a vast host of demons.

To him, under God, was committed upon the earth the power of death. Cast out of heaven as his proper sphere and "proper abode," he still has access to God as the "accuser of our brethren" and is permitted a certain power of sitting or testing the self-confident and carnal among believers; but this is a strictly permissive and limited power, and believers so sifted are kept in faith through the advocacy of Christ.

At the beginning of the great tribulation Satan's privilege of access to God as accuser will be withdrawn. At the return of Christ in glory Satan will be bound for 1000 years, after which he will be "released for a short time" and will become the head of a final effort to overthrow the kingdom. Defeated in this, he will be cast into the lake of fire, his final doom. The notion that he reigns in hell is not Biblical. He (is prince of this present world system but) will be tormented in the lake of fire. (*New Scofield Study Bible*, pg. 1798)

> *Now the serpent was more crafty than any of the wild animals the LORD God had made. He said to the woman, "Did God really say, 'You must not eat from any tree in the garden?" The woman said to the serpent, "We may eat fruit from the trees in the garden, but God did say, 'You must not eat fruit from the tree that is in the middle of the garden, and you must not touch it, or you*

will die.'" "You will surely not die," the serpent said to the woman. "For God knows that when you eat of it your eyes will be opened, and you will be like God, knowing good and evil." When the woman saw that the fruit of the tree was good for food and pleasing to the eye, and also desirable for gaining wisdom, she took some and ate it. She also gave some to her husband, who was with her, and he ate it. **Genesis 3:1–6**

The serpent, in his form in Eden, is not to be thought of as a writhing reptile. That is the effect of the curse. The creature which lent itself to Satan may well have been the most beautiful of all creatures that were less than man. Traces of beauty remain despite the curse. Every movement of a serpent is graceful, and many species are beautifully colored. The curse moves the serpent from the most beautiful and subtle creatures to one of the most loathsome creatures. (*New Scofield Study Bible*, pg. 98)

Satan is disguised as a crafty serpent, yet there is no indication that Eve was concerned with his presence. She shows no alarm when the serpent speaks to her. Temptation is Satan's invitation to give in to his kind of life. Notice that what the serpent said to Eve was a lie but only partially. Every lie then and now has an element of truth in it, which made it all the more deceptive.

Satan can always find a tool adapted to the work he has in hand, and is an indication of our danger. There is no instrument so feeble, that Satan cannot use to tempt us.

How can we resist temptation? First, realize being tempted is not a sin. Then, pray for strength to resist, sometimes run; sometimes we have the idea that freedom is doing what we want. However, freedom comes from obedience to God and by knowing what is right and wrong, good and evil. When we leave God out of our plans, we are placing ourselves above God. This is exactly what Satan wants us to do. Our sins do not always appear ugly to us. Use God's Word and God's people to help stand against temptation and sin.

One day the angels came to present themselves before the LORD, and Satan also came with them. The LORD said to Satan, "Where have you come from?" Satan answered the LORD, "From roaming through the earth going back and forth in it." Then the LORD said to Satan, "Have you considered my servant Job? There is no one on earth like him; he is blameless and upright, a man who fears God and shuns evil." "Does Job fear God for nothing?" Satan replied. "Have you not put a hedge around him and his household and everything he has? You have blessed the work of his hands, so that his flocks and herds are spread throughout the land. But stretch out your hand and strike everything he has, and he will surely curse you to your face." The LORD said to Satan, "Very well, then, everything he has is in your hands, but on the man himself do not lay a finger." **Job 1:6–9**

Satan has full access to heaven and seems to be the cynic of heaven. The material possessions surrounding Jobs life, according to Satan, are sufficient explanations of his righteousness. Remove these and the righteousness will disappear. Satan is claiming that prosperity is the root of Job's faith, remove the root and the blossom will die.

When God asks Satan if he has he considered his servant Job, this was not to increase God's information, but to alert the angels that were present to hear and have their attention called to the doings of Satan. These doings would need to be watched by them, and sometimes to be restrained or prevented.

Job doesn't know the reasons for his suffering but he has learned to trust God no matter what. It was then that his faith could fully develop. Remember we live in a world where good is not always rewarded and sin and evil punished. To be unshakable, faith must be built on confidence that God's purpose will be fulfilled. Like Job, we should take time daily to pray. Remember Satan is accountable to God, Satan can only be at one place at a time, his demons aid him but both are limited. God's people can overcome Satan through God's power.

One day the angels came to present themselves before the LORD, and Satan also came with them, to present himself before him. And the LORD said to Satan, "Where have you come from?" Satan answered the LORD, "From roaming through the earth going back and forth in it." Then the LORD said to Satan, "Have you considered my servant Job? There is no one on earth like him; he is blameless and upright, a man who fears God and shuns evil. And he still maintains his integrity, though you incited me against him to ruin him without any reason." "Skin for skin!" Satan replied. "A man will give all he has for his own life. But stretch out our hand and strike his flesh and bones, and he will surely curse you to your face." The LORD said to Satan, "Very well, then, he is in your hands; but you must spare his life." **Job 2:1-6**

On the first occasion, Satan came only to observe and was addressed by God. This time the words are added, "And Satan came also." Satan's power is under God's control, and extends only as far as God allows.

Satan came before the LORD but God was not fooled, he understood that Satan will slander mankind in hopes of turning God against us. However, God will only allow Satan so much latitude against us. Satan is seldom satisfied with only one attempt against the virtue of Christians. He is unwilling to admit himself defeated in spiritual conflicts. God may allow us to be tried by Satan, but He does not cease to love us. God may listen to the charges Satan makes against us, but He doesn't believe them.

"See, I set before you today life and prosperity, death and destruction. This day I call heaven and earth as witness against you that I have set before you life and death, blessings and curses. Now choose life, so that you and your children may live. **Deuteronomy 30: 15, 19**

There are three kinds of curses: These are curses from God, legal curses from Satan, and illegal curses from Satan. The first two can only be broken by repentance of sins. The third is easily broken in the name of Jesus. There are two purposes for curses. Curses from or by Satan are for the purpose of injury, destruction, loss and death. Curses sent by God are to get attention and to turn that person to God.

In today's world we have a clear understanding of inherited conditions, physical and emotional. But we almost never consider the possibility of inherited spiritual curses or family sins. Most of us know very little about activities or actions or blessings or curses of grandparents or great-grandparents. The sins of the past can have devastating effects on our own lives. How do we change

47

this effect and the power of Satan and demons have over us. Confess the sins of our forefathers and ask the Lord for forgiveness and cleansing. Ask the Lord to separate us from the sins of our forefathers.

If you find that you have trouble with some types of prayer by way of confusion, lack of any ability to concentrate on or during the prayer, or are so tongue twisted you cannot say the words, the demons are strenuously fighting against your breaking the curse. Don't give in; go step by step through the prayer until you can do so easily and freely.

We do not need to walk in fear. We have immense power and freedom in Christ. However, we do need to walk wisely and in harmony with God's Word. (Anderson, *The Bondage Breaker*, Chapter 3, pgs. 41–56)

God doesn't force His will on us. He lets us decide whether to follow Him or reject Him. This decision, however, is a life or death matter. God wants us to realize this, for he would like us all to choose life. We have to decide daily to follow Him and His commandments. Sometimes we feel these commandments are too hard. We have no excuses, obeying God as Christians is reasonable, sensible, and beneficial. The most difficult part of obeying God is simply the decision to start now. (*Life Application Bible*, pg. 321)

"They are to teach my people the difference between the holy and the common and show them how to distinguish between the unclean and the clean." **Ezekiel 44:23**

We have little knowledge of those things that the Lord proclaims to be unclean. Thus our lives and homes are cluttered with unclean things which enable curses and demons to operate in our lives. (Anderson, *The Bondage Breaker*, Chapter 10, pgs. 153–170)

Then Jesus was led by the Spirit into the desert to be tempted by the devil. After fasting forty days and forty nights, he was hungry. The tempter came to him and said, "If you are the Son of God, tell these stones to become bread." Jesus answered, "It is written: 'Man does not live on bread alone, but on every word that comes from the mouth of God." Then the devil took him to the holy city and had him stand on the highest point of the temple. "If you are the Son of God," he said, "throw yourself down. For it is written: "He will command his angels concerning you, and they will lift you in their hands, so that you will not strike your foot against a stone."' Jesus answered him, "It is also written: 'Do not put the Lord your God to the test.'" Again, the devil took him to a very high mountain and showed him all the kingdoms of the world and their splendor. "All this I will give you," he said, "if you will bow down and worship me." Jesus said to him, "Away from me, Satan! For it is written: "Worship the Lord your God, and serve him only."' Then the devil left him, and angels came and attended him.
Matthew 4:1–11

Matthew named Satan "the tempter" when Satan confronted Jesus in the wilderness. Also the apostle Paul referred to Satan as "the tempter" (1 Thessalonians 3:5). This name describes his work that began after his own fall and will continue until he is cast into the lake of fire. This name highlights one of Satan's major activities, tempting others to sin. (Lightner, *Angels, Satan, and Demons*, pg. 76)

The devil spoke a challenge to Jesus "if you are . . ." in other words, "prove you are . . ." Jesus answered the devil with Scripture. Humans live on the Word of God. The devil took Jesus to "church." A favorite place for the devil to tempt, disrupt, and divide is within the church. The devil knows scripture. He spoke scripture back to Jesus. The scripture comes from Psalm 91:11–12. Notice the devil left out the line that read, "To guard you in all your ways." The devil quotes the parts of scripture that meet his purposes. Jesus lost his temper with the devil, "away. . . ." he shouted. (Rogerson, *The Angels of God*, handout, 3)

> But when Jesus turned and looked at his disciples, he rebuked Peter, "Get behind me, Satan" he said, "You do not have in mind the things of God, but the things of men." **Mark 8:33**

Satan tempted Jesus to avoid the way of the cross; here he uses the Disciples, especially Peter to try tempting again. It is thought here that Jesus recognizes the voice of Satan as the one he heard in the wilderness. Satan's motives were evil; the disciples however were motivated by love. Look closely at your own motives and God's will and listen for an indication from God as to His will.

There are so many subtle claims that Satan uses to draw us from being Christ centered. These can be hard to discern. We must measure each message by the Word of God to see if it is God's truth. Peter spoke from his worldly view of the Messiah. How often have we spoken without thinking it through clearly?

If someone has taken offense at us, we should seek a resolution to the offense. Apologize or whatever the situation requires (*Standard Lesson Commentary 2002–2003*, pg.321).

When the devil had finished all this tempting, he left him until an opportune time. **Luke 4:13**

The Greek original translation "all the temptation" would be more accurately translated "every kind of temptation." The every day lesson, which we may read into this story, is that from the path of God's will before us, no persuasion, however skillfully worded, should be sufficient to turn us away from God. The tempter departed from Jesus for a season; more accurately, till a convenient time. All through the two and a half years of his public ministry, Jesus was exposed to the various trials and temptations that we are also exposed. However, the "convenient season" here probably refers to that other great temptation just before the cross, when our Lord prayed in the agony of the garden. The devil clearly comes back throughout Jesus ministry. Notice that **Satan knows scripture**. However, he misinterprets it for his own ends.

Jesus said to them, "If God were your Father, you would love me, for I came from God and now am here. I have not come on my own; but he sent me. Why is my language not clear to you? Because you are unable to hear what I say. You belong to your father, the devil, and you want to carry out your father's desire. He was a murderer from the beginning, not holding to the truth, for there is no truth in him. When he lies, he speaks his native language, for he is a liar and the father of lies. Yet, because I tell the truth, you do not believe me! Can any of you prove me guilty of sin? If I am telling the truth, why don't you believe me? He who belongs to God hears what God says, 'The reason you do not hear is that you do not belong to God.' **John 8:42–47**

The purpose the devil and his demons have for lying is to deceive. Those who listen to their lies stand in danger of believing what they say. The speaking of demons is never motivated by a desire to help us; the demons are laying snares. For us to listen to them with the intention of sorting out any truth that they might utter, could be compared to drinking water with poison in it with an intention of filtering out the poison with our teeth. (Hammond, *Demons and Deliverance*, pg. 20)

Satan hates the truth. He lies, and so expresses his true nature. Satan used the religious leader's stubbornness, pride and prejudices to keep them from believing. The leader's hatred of truth, lies and murderous intentions shows how much Satan had control over them. Attitudes and actions show whose we are, either Satan or Christ. Satan still uses his lies, and hate to obstruct God's work.

———————

If anyone has caused grief, he has not so much grieved me as he has grieved all of you, to some extent, not to put it too severely. The punishment inflicted on him by the majority is sufficient for him. Now instead, you ought to forgive and comfort him, so that he will not be overwhelmed by excessive sorrow. I urge you, therefore, to reaffirm your love for him. The reason I wrote to you was to see if you would stand the test and be obedient in everything. If you forgive anyone, I also forgive him. And what I have forgiven, if there was anything to forgive, I have forgiven in the sight of Christ for your sake, in order that Satan might not outwit us. For we are not unaware of his schemes. **2 Corinthians 2:5–11**

When the church punishes sinners, they need to remember the concept of forgiveness. After repentance and a changing of life and actions, we need also to forgive. Church discipline should seek restoration. Lack of forgiveness gives Satan an advantage and an opening. Satan can try to harm the church by tempting us to use discipline in an unforgiving way. Remember Satan has a mind and can use it against us.

For such men are false apostles, deceitful workmen, masquerading as apostles of Christ. And no wonder, for Satan himself masquerades as an angel of light. It is not surprising, then, if his servants masquerade as servants of righteousness. Their end will be what their actions deserve. **2 Corinthians 11:13–15**

The New Testament teaches us that we have an active spiritual adversary in this world, namely Satan; and that he enslaves people to be his ministers. Their "gospel" would be as a "gospel of righteousness" in order to trap the unwary. It is essential for all who would be truly saved to know that righteousness comes to us only through faith in Jesus Christ, not of our own works. Satan and his servants can deceive us by appearing to be attractive, good and moral. Those who are unsuspecting can be deceived into following smooth talking Bible quoting leaders. External appearances are not accurate indications of who belongs to Christ. We need to ask; do the teachings proclaim and affirm that Jesus was the Son of God who came into this world to save us from our sins?

Therefore, put on the full armor of God, so that when the day of evil comes, you may be able to stand your ground, and after you have done everything, to stand.
Ephesians 6:13

Satan and his demons are not fantasies. They are very real. They will use every device possible to turn us away from Christ and back to him. The enemies of the soul are neither earthly forces, nor beings on a level with man, but are the leaders of the evil spiritual forces of the universe. For spiritual warfare, weapons are essential, and without them, there can be no withstanding the powers of evil. The Word of God and prayer are linked together and should be used together in this warfare. Prayer is to be used in respect to everything, with the added guidance of the Holy Spirit.

. . . and that they will come to their senses and escape from the trap of the devil, who has taken them captive to do his will. **2 Timothy 2:6**

Those who have been taken alive by the devil through teaching and patient instruction may return to awareness, escape from the snare of Satan, and enter into the pursuit of God's will. In this scripture, you can see that Satan, like us, has a will. He wants people to do his will, create destruction, diversions, and create trouble.

Then the dragon was enraged at the woman and went off to make war against the rest of her offspring, those who obey God's commandments and hold to the testimony of Jesus. **Revelation 12:17**

Webster's Dictionary defines a dragon as "a huge serpent" or "a fabulous animal generally represented as a monstrous winged and scaly serpent or saurian with a crested head and enormous claws." To call Satan a dragon suggests his power and strength and the vast devastation he is capable of causing. John saw Satan as a red dragon with seven heads and ten horns, who with the demons of hell were arrayed against the Lord and His people. (Revelation 12:3–4, 9–12, 16–17). (Lightner, *Angels, Satan, and Demons,* pg. 76)

Here we see the power of Satan's emotions. He is enraged. A horrific spiritual battle is going on. God will win the war, but we battle daily, don't waiver in your commitment to Christ.

Names Used For Satan/
Demons/Fallen Angels

Names were important in Bible times for they were character-revealing. This is true of the names ascribed to God, humans, and both good and evil angels. Satan's names are descriptive of his person and his work.

Satan is the name most often used for the archenemy of God and humans. In Hebrew the word for Satan means "adversary." This is his true character. The Old Testament mentions Satan eighteen times. The New Testament mentions Satan thirty four times in twelve books.

(Lightner, *Angels, Satan, and Demons*, pg. 73)

> *Then he showed me Joshua the high priest standing before the angel of the LORD, and Satan standing at his right side to **accuse** him. The LORD said to Satan, "LORD rebuke you, Satan!" The LORD, who has chosen Jerusalem, rebuke you! Is not this man a burning stick snatched from the fire?* **Zechariah 3:1–2**

The angel of the LORD and Satan are together. The LORD rebuked Satan. Satan is always accusing people of their sins, but he truly does not understand the depth and breadth of God's forgiveness and mercy. Satan is cunning and strong, maliciously working as he has done from the beginning, to keep us apart from God. Nevertheless, his power is usurped, and his devices are doomed to defeat. He may work toward giving us a guilty conscience but it is not to lead to repentance, but increase our fear and distrust and to widen the breach between God and us. If he can make us believe we are too sinful to be forgiven, he wins. We can rebuke Satan ourselves or we can ask God to do it for us. When Satan makes you feel dirty and unworthy, remember that through the blood of Christ you are washed clean and worthy to draw near to God.

Many will say to me on that day, 'Lord, Lord, did we not prophesy in your name, and in your name drive out demons and perform many miracles?' **Matthew 7:22**

Every age has had "hangers on" who make outward profession of faith, but are insincere and self-seeking. It is possible, but dangerous, to have some sort of relationship with the Lord Jesus Christ which does not include salvation. Profession without possession is a real danger. Sinful conduct is the evidence of an unregenerate heart. There is no middle course. We either gather souls for Christ or scatter them from God.

There are those who are "religious" but have no relationship to Christ. On judgment day, only our acceptance of Christ as Lord and Savior and obedience will matter. We are responsible as leaders to teach this simple truth.

A student is not above his teacher, nor a servant above his master. It is easy enough for the student to be like his teacher, and the servant like his master. If the head of the house has been called Beelzebub, how much more the members of his household. So do not be afraid of them.

> *There is nothing concealed that will not be disclosed, or hidden that will not be made known. What I tell you in the dark, speak in the daylight; what is whispered in your ear, proclaim from the roofs.* **Matthew 10:24–27**

The Pharisees used this name to describe the ruler of the demons or Satan when they tried to explain how Jesus cast out demons. The name Beelzebul perhaps derives from Baal-Zebub, god of the Philistine city of Ekron. Beel-Zebub means "lord of the flies," and Beelzebul comes from a Hebrew construction meaning "Lord of filth." These two words, then are suggestive of flies swarming over the trash heap outside the city of Jerusalem. (Lightner, *Angels, Satan, and Demons,* pg. 74)

God is sometimes labeled evil. If Jesus was called evil what will we be called? When persecution is experienced we must not fear. Three times Jesus tells his disciples not to be afraid, to strengthen them against the temptation of fear. He teaches us that as disciples we should anticipate opposition and persecution. There is a price to pay for being a follower of Jesus.

Everything covered and hid shall eventually be brought to light. The teachings He had given us is truth. Even though it was received privately, it must be shouted from the housetops. Evil and error are to be judged and defeated by the light of truth. Fear is the enemy of boldness. Fear of man will rob Christ's servants of their boldness to proclaim His truth. Faithfulness to God is more important than life itself. It is better to die than to deny. Therefore, reverential fear of God must replace one's cringing fear of man.

The disciples reward is with God. He knows each hair of our heads, and He knows the condition of each little sparrow. We are valuable in the sight of God. Truth divides. There will always be those who are unteachable. (Hammond, Demons and Deliverance, pg. 96)

———————————

Then they brought him a demon-possessed man who was blind and mute, and Jesus healed him, so that he could both talk and see. All the people were astonished and said, "Could this be the Son of David?" But when the Pharisees heard this, they said, "It is only by Beelzebub, the prince of demons, that this fellow drives out demons.
Matthew 12:22–24

These verses remind us that we face an enemy who does not play games. He is relentless, he never gives up. Jesus' power over demons shows that Satan was already bound. God knows our thoughts, our motives. Jesus has complete power and authority over Satan and demons.

———————————

When an evil spirit comes out of a man, it goes through arid places seeking rest and does not find it. Then it says, "I will return to the house I left." When it arrives, it finds the house unoccupied, swept clean and put in order. Then it goes and takes with it seven other spirits more wicked than itself, and they go in and live there. And the final condition of that man is worse than the first. That is how it will be with this wicked generation.
Matthew 12:43–45

When evil spirits are driven out of a person, a spiritual condition is created which Jesus compares to a newly vacated house.

He taught that if the life is left unoccupied, it is susceptible to the return of the old tenant and his friends. (Hammond, *Demons and Deliverance*, pg. 17)

If a person only gets free from some demonic affliction and fails to fill up his life with the Word and the Holy Spirits fullness, he/she well may face worse problems ahead than what he had before the bold confrontation. Cleaning up one's life without filling it with God and the Holy Spirit makes us easy marks for Satan.

He answered, "The one who sowed the good seed is the Son of Man. The field is the world, and the good seed stands for the sons of the kingdom. The weeds are the sons of the evil one, and the enemy who sows them is the devil. The harvest is the end of the age, and the harvesters are angels. **Matthew 13:37–39**

"Devil" is the second most common name for the head of the fallen angels. It occurs in the New Testament thirty-six times. It describes his character, just as "Satan" does. The name "devil" translates the Greek diabolos, from a verb meaning "to throw." It is clear from this that the devil hurls accusations; he slanders, tears down, or defames God to man and man to God.

Today in churches, there are true believers and false believers, but only God is qualified to be the judge. If we judge, we can damage others. We can only judge our own true-ness and responses to God's call.

> *Now is the time for judgment on this world; now the*
> *prince of this world will be driven out.* **John 12:31**

When Satan fell because of his sin, he instituted a counter-kingdom. He rules the cosmos, the world or orderly system of wicked angels and unregenerated humans. This counter-kingdom over which Satan rules is the opposite of and stands in defiance of God's rule. Three times Jesus used this name for Satan, calling him "the ruler of this world" (John 12:31, 14:30; 16:11).

The apostle Paul called Satan a "prince" as he described the Ephesian Christians' hopeless condition before they came to faith in Christ. They "formerly walked according to the course of this world, according to the prince of the power of the air" (Ephesians 2:2). In the same sentence Paul referred to Satan as "the spirit that is now working in the sons of disobedience." Though those outside of Christ may not be aware of it, Satan is at work in their minds and emotions, seeking to keep them from trusting Christ. This parallels the spiritual blindness Paul referred to when he wrote to the Corinthian Christians (2 Corinthians 4:4). Though Satan is the ruler or the prince of the world system that opposes God, his empire or rule is limited. He is not sovereign as God is. All Satan does is under the wise permission of God Himself and for His own good purposes. (Lightner, *Angels, Satan, and Demons*, pg. 75)

This judgment refers to Jesus Christ as bearing the believer's sins, which have been judged in the person of Jesus Christ "lifted up" on the cross. The result was death for Christ and justification for the believer, who can never again be put in jeopardy. *(New Scofield Bible*, pg. 1503)

The prince of the world is Satan. Satan is real, not symbolic and works against those who obey God. Jesus appeals to us to walk in the light and to believe in the light. He warns it is possible to walk in darkness and reject the light.

I will not speak with you much longer, for the prince of this world is coming. He has no hold on me, but the world must learn that I love the Father and that I do exactly what my Father has commanded me. "Come now; let us leave." **John 14:30–31**

Sin, fear, uncertainty, doubt and numerous forces are at war within us. God can restrain these hostile forces and give us peace if we accept it from him. If we obey Jesus and align ourselves closely with God's purposes, Satan can have no power over us.

For I am convinced that neither death nor life, neither angels nor demons, neither the present nor the future, nor any powers, neither height nor depth, nor anything else in all creation, will be able to separate us from the love of God that is in Christ Jesus our Lord. **Romans 8:38**

Christ has conquered all enemies and put them under his feet. This is the promise that God has given us in Christ. These verses contain one of the most comforting promises in all Scripture. Believers have always had to face hardships in many forms: persecution, illness, imprisonment, even death. These could cause them to fear that they have been abandoned by Christ. Paul exclaims that it is impossible to be separated from Christ. His death for us is proof of his unconquerable love. Nothing can stop Christ's constant presence with us. God tells us how great his love is so that we will feel totally secure in him. If we believe these overwhelming assurances, we will not be afraid.

"Powers" are unseen forces of evil in our world, like Satan and his demons. In Christ we are protected from such forces, but we need to claim this power through the blood and in the name of Christ. (*Life Application Bible*, pg. 2043)

We must remember that the powers of darkness do not make all their attacks in the open, with the noise and confusion of open conflict. The devil is too wise for this. He likes to bushwhack God's people, surprise them, and catch them off guard. The devil likes to administer opiates to God's people. Under the guise of superior knowledge, and culture, he likes to whisper to us that we should forget about sin; that, after all, it is not such a bad thing; it is only the growing pains that come with growing up. As long as it doesn't hurt anyone else, what's the problem?

———

The god of this age has blinded the minds of unbelievers, so that they cannot see the light of the gospel of the glory of Christ, who is the image of God. **2 Corinthians 4:4**

As "the god of this world," Satan heads up an anti-God philosophy that permeates the thinking of the unsaved. Satan "has blinded the minds of the unbelieving, that they might not see the light of the gospel of the glory of Christ." This means all unbelievers are supernaturally blinded to their need of Christ and His power to redeem. Only the supernatural power of the Holy Spirit can remove that blindness. He does just that through the Word which we are to proclaim.

As God's ambassadors we have the privilege and responsibility of sharing the good news of God's saving grace in Christ. We must remember though we cannot convict sinners of their need of Christ; neither can we redeem them. The Holy Spirit alone convicts of sin, draws the sinner, shows the unsaved his or her need of Christ, and enables the sinner to believe. (Lightner, *Angels, Satan, and Demons,* pg. 75)

Satan is the "god of this age." His work is to deceive. Satan uses the allure of the world's offerings to blind people to Christ (Life Application Bible, pg. 2097).

The work of the "god of this world" is directed towards the object of turning men away from the light. Sin has marred the image of God in us; but it can be made perfect again through Jesus Christ.

As for you, you were dead in your transgressions and sins, in which you used to live when you followed the ways of this world and of the ruler of the kingdom of the air, the spirit who is now at work in those who are disobedient. All of us also lived among them at one time, gratifying the cravings of our sinful nature and following its desires and thoughts. Like the rest, we were by nature objects of wrath. But because of his great love for us, God, who is rich in mercy, made us alive with Christ even when we were dead in transgressions, it is by grace you have been saved. Ephesians 2:1–5

Spiritual death is the state of the natural person who is still in their sins, alienated from the life of God, and destitute of the Spirit. Prolonged beyond the death of the body, spiritual death is a state of eternal separation from God in conscious suffering.

Satan's is not a supreme authority, but an authority used by permission from God. Because this evil has for so long been the rule among natural man, it is unrecognized and counted as simply "human nature." But the spiritual forces of evil are in control of the natural man. Mercy and love were the elements that moved God to help us. The blessing bestowed upon us by the work of Christ is that of new life. It is only in our union with Christ that we have new life, and we are raised with Christ.

We are lost in sin and cannot save ourselves. "Objects of wrath" refers to those who are to receive God's wrath because of their rejection of Christ. We no longer need to live under sin's power and the old sinful nature. The penalty of sin and the power of sin over us is destroyed by Christ on the cross. We still feel like sinning, and sometimes we will sin. The difference is we are not dead in sin and slaves to our sinful natures, but are alive in Christ and his power.

Knowing our spiritual weaknesses and the potential for evil in us is absolutely essential if we are to avoid the snare of Satan. We will never be prepared to avoid the snares of Satan unless and until we acknowledge our capacity and inner desire to sin. Of course Satan knows all our weak points and always attacks where he knows he can gain the best foothold (Lightner, *Angels, Satan, and Demons,* pg. 80).

Have nothing to do with the fruitless deeds of darkness, but rather expose them. For it is shameful even to mention what the disobedient do in secret.
Ephesians 5:11–12

By questioning everything, the Christian can avoid being

deceived, and come to know the will of God. However, we are to go beyond the avoidance of the works of darkness, but also to expose the influence evil has in our lives. There are so many evils that we are exposed to in subtle attempts to clutter our minds and distract our hearts away from Christ. Not only is it important to avoid pleasures that lead to sin; we must go further. We must take a stand for what is right and good.

For he has rescued us from the dominion of darkness
and brought us into the kingdom of the Son he loves,
in whom we have redemption, the forgiveness of sins.
Colossians 1:13

The believer is part of this kingdom and no longer subject to the powers of darkness. These Christians feared the unforeseen forces of darkness, but true believers have been transferred to light, freedom, forgiveness, and from the power of Satan to the power of God. Our conduct should reflect our allegiance (*Living Application Bible*, pg. 2159). We need to give Christ first place in all our thoughts and activities.

Be self-controlled and alert. Your enemy the devil prowls
around like a roaring lion looking for someone to devour.
1 Peter 5:8

Peter expresses the hostility of the devil to Christians and our life in Christ as well as the methods of false accusations and slander, which Satan employs. The use of the lion depicts the strength and destructiveness of our adversary.

Satan is like a lion looking for someone to devour: the weak, the young, the struggling Christian. The devil can come not just as a lion but also as a dove or a purring tabby cat, assuring us that everything is all right; that we need not be so careful, that there is no danger, that a little poetic license here and there will do no harm. We need to cultivate a spirit that is sensitive to evil. We need to watch during the times we feel alone, weak, helpless, and cut off from other believers. We cannot become so focused on our own troubles that we do not watch for danger. It is during these times that we should walk even closer in fellowship with other Christians. We can help each other resist the devil. We need that sharing of Jesus, support and fellowship.

Peter said the way believers are to respond to Satan is to "resist" him while being firm in faith. Before the terse description of the devil's maneuvers the saints were told, "Humble yourselves, therefore, under the mighty hand of God" and cast "all your anxiety upon Him." These Christian graces enable believers to be successful in resisting Satan. (Lightner, *Angels, Satan, and Demons,* pg. 79)

Do not be like Cain, who belonged to the evil one and murdered his brother. And why did he murder him? Because his own actions were evil and his brother's were righteous. Do not be surprised, my brothers, if the world hates you. We know that we have passed from death to life, because we love our brothers. Anyone who does not love remains in death. Anyone who hates his brother is a murderer, and you know that no murderer has eternal life in him. **1 John 3:12–15**

Wickedness always hates the goodness. Goodness shows what should be, and we ought not to be surprised when the world rejects us. But if the world hates; as Christians we are to love. When we have come to realize the greatness of God's love for us, we have an obligation to give love to others. People who try to be upright and righteous shame those who are not. Hate is murder; outward compliance to Christ without inward regeneration is not enough. Hate is a cancer that Satan can use to devour us. This bitter root can grow in a church and eventually destroy it (*Life Application Bible,* pg. 2280).

We know that we are children of God, and that the whole world is under the control of the evil one. **1 John 5:19**

In calling Satan "the evil one" Jesus and John both depicted him as totally corrupt and carrying on a corrupt and evil work (John 17:15). Evil beyond description, Satan personally seeks to influence the whole world toward wickedness, just as he did with Cain (1 John 3:12). But believers, John affirmed, are exempt from this awful grip of Satan (John 5:18). This evil one, John wrote, can be overcome by the Word of God (John 2:13–14). There is no middle ground with Christ, we either believe and belong to Christ and obey him or we live under Satan's control (*Life Application Bible,* pg. 2284).

The Power of Satan and
How He Uses That Power

Do not underestimate Satan or his demons. If they were truly stupid and incompetent, they would never have made such successful inroads into human nature, nor would there be so much evil and corruption in this world. The devil can argue, the devil can reason, the devil can negotiate with the best of them. According to Catholic teaching, the demons were "pure" impure spirits, highly intelligent and self-motivated. Their will was bent on evil, on corrupting and damning mankind, but the methods they used were singular and in many instances remarkably creative. (Masello, *Fallen Angels*, pg. 60)

It is a common problem of those under attack of Satan to become preoccupied with thoughts about how Satan is tempting, afflicting, or oppressing them rather than meditating on the victory Christ has won in their lives. Dr. A.W. Tozer in his book, "Born After Midnight" brings perspective to this:

> *The scriptural way to see things is to set the Lord always before us, put Christ in the center of our vision, and if Satan is lurking around he will appear on the margin only and be seen as but a shadow on the edge of the brightness. It is always wrong to reverse this—to set Satan in the focus of our vision and push God out to the margin. Nothing but tragedy can come of such inversion.*

A snare is "something by which one is entangled, involved

in difficulties, held fast, or impeded . . . something deceptively attractive." This description fits Satan perfectly. When we know the biblical picture of him, we are better prepared to avoid his snares. (Lightner, *Angels, Satan, and Demons*, pg. 78)

The best way to keep the enemy out is to keep Christ in. The sheep need not be terrified by the world; they have but to stay close to the shepherd. It is not the praying sheep Satan fears, but the presence of the shepherd.

The instructed Christian whose faculties have been developed by the Word and the Spirit will not fear the devil. When necessary he/she will stand against the power of darkness and overcome them by the blood of the Lamb and the word of his/her testimony. He will recognize the peril in which he lives and will know what to do about it, but he will practice the presence of God and never allow himself to become devil-conscious.

Satan rose up against Israel and **incited** *David to take a census of Israel. So David said to Joab and the commanders of the troops, "Go and count the Israelites from Beersheba to Dan. Then report back to me so that I may know how many there are."* **I Chronicles 21:1–2**

What is wrong with taking a census? Shouldn't David know how many troops he has to take into battle? Herein lays the subtlety of Satan. Satan wanted David to rely on his own resources rather than Gods. How did Satan incite David? He used David's thoughts. These thoughts come in such a way we think they are our own. Sometimes this comes as difficulty concentrating or as staying awake when reading the Bible. If it is a condemning thought, we have difficulty refocusing on some other subject or thought. We each have self-talk from our past. With practice we can learn to discern what our negative talk is and which is Satan attempting to incite us with his thoughts? We can learn to shut off our own negative talk to ourselves. Thoughts that Satan puts into our minds can only be stopped with prayer and rebuke of Satan.

Satan incited David with the sin of pride. Satan cannot force people to do wrong—only tempt them with the idea. Temptation is not the sin; acting on the temptation is the sin. An action may in itself not be sinful but the motivation behind it can be the sin. We must constantly weigh our motives before we act. Self-sufficiency pulls us away from God.

From that time on Jesus began to explain to his disciples that he must go to Jerusalem and suffer many things at the hands of the elders, chief priests and teachers of the law, and that he must be killed on the third day be raised to life. Peter took him aside and began to rebuke him. "Never, Lord!" he said. "This shall never happen to you!" Jesus turned and said to Peter, "Get behind me Satan! You are a stumbling block to me; you do not have in mind the things of God, but the things of men."
Matthew 16:21–23

Immediately after Peter's declaration of faith, he evaluates the situation in human terms. Peter's instantaneous reaction to our Lord's new teaching shows how foreign to our way of thinking the concept of suffering is.

There is a mixture in man. The same Peter who moments earlier spoke by divine revelation became the mouthpiece of Satan.

We must recognize that every human is fallible. It is dangerous to elevate anyone, however much they have been used of God and however much truth they have proclaimed.

Many leaders have become "popes" in the eyes of their followers. The problem then becomes if false doctrine is preached, the whole following goes over the cliff together. The Bible is the criteria for judging every person's message. No one has full insights into the things of God. Even Peter was used of Satan and spoke contrary to the Word of God. (Hammond, *Demons and Deliverance,* pg 107)

Satan is always trying to get us to leave God out; here Jesus rebukes Peter for the attitude.

> *So Jesus called them and spoke to them in parables: How can Satan drive out Satan? If a kingdom is divided against itself, that kingdom cannot stand. If a house is divided against itself, that house cannot stand. And if Satan opposes himself and is divided, he cannot stand; his end has come. In fact, no one can enter a strong man's house and carry off his possessions unless he first ties up the strong man. Then he can rob his house."* **Mark 3:23–27**

Jesus shows the absurdity of such an allegation and then warns of the awful consequences that would result. There is nothing more illogical than unbelief. There is a graduation from kingdom, to house, to Satan. We need to remember that the smaller a community of faith, the more fatal the division. The Pharisees refused to believe the power of Jesus came from God, because they would have to accept Jesus as the Messiah (*Life Application Bible,* pg. 1733). Their sin was pride. Jesus, because he is God, has power over Satan. As long as Satan can keep us in the darkness of ignorance: ignorance of God; of Christ; of the way of salvation; of ourselves, of our slavery; of our responsibility; of our danger; and of our duty, he is secure in his possession of us. By subtly, wiles, and wickedness he holds possession of the inner recesses of our hearts, actually furnishing them with his delusions. Jesus has the power to overcome all of Satan's delusions. The Word of God gives us power over Satan.

Ekketion

"The farmer sows the word. Some people are like seed along the path, where the word is sown. As soon as they hear it, Satan comes and takes away the word that was sown in them. Others, like seed sown on rocky places, hear the word and at once receive it with joy. But since they have no root, they last only a short time. When trouble or persecution comes because of the word, they quickly fall away. Still others, like seed sown among thorns, hear the word; but the worries of this life, the deceitfulness of wealth and the desires for other things come in and choke the word, making it unfruitful. Others, like seed sown on good soil, hear the word, accept it, and produce a crop—thirty, sixty, or even a hundred times what was sown." Mark 4:14–20

Jesus taught the existence of a personal power of evil. There are things that hinder the reception of the word such as hard hearted indifference, pre-occupation with the cares and riches of the world, and lack of spiritual depth. This scripture is not just four different kinds of people, but different times in our lives, how we can accept Jesus in part of our lives but not in others. Satan can speak to steal seeds through materialism, false sense of security, allowing our lives to become over crowded so we can't hear God's voice. Warned by Scripture, we are called to consider how we hear. We must beware of being turned aside from the path of duty, from the study of God's Word, from prayer or from the worship in the sanctuary, or from service of any kind. We need to earnestly seek the aid of the Holy Spirit to preserve us from any evil, and unbelief in which the seed of God's Word cannot take root and grow.

He shouted at the top of his voice, "What do you want with me, Jesus, Son of the Most High God? Swear to God that you won't torture me!" **Mark 5:7**

Demons are best able to do their work when they can conceal their presence and identity. They work under a cover of darkness. It is a severe blow to them when their presence and nature are revealed. (Hammond, *Demons and Deliverance*, pg. 22)

"Teacher," said John, "we saw a man driving out demons in your name and we told him to stop, because he was not one of us." "Do not stop him," Jesus said. "No one who does a miracle in my name can in the next moment say anything bad about me, for whoever is not against us is for us. I tell you the truth, anyone who gives you a cup of water in my name because you belong to Christ will certainly not lose his reward." **Mark 9:38–41**

We cannot be truly neutral about Christ. Matthew 12:30 says, "He who is not with us is against me." However, his followers will not all resemble each other. People who are "on Jesus' side" have the same goal of building up the kingdom, and we should not let our differences interfere with this goal.

"Then should not this woman, a daughter of Abraham, whom Satan has kept bound for eighteen long years, be set free on the Sabbath day from what bound her?" Luke 13:16

Pharisees use law to avoid the obligation of love. Disease and disability are common in today's world. Every possible consideration was shown in cases of their own interests; no mercy was to be considered, though, where the sick or the poor were concerned. Christ vividly draws a contrast between animals and humans.

The causes are many but can be a direct attack of Satan. Jesus is more powerful than Satan or any disease. He may or may not give physical healing but on His return, He will put an end to ALL diseases and disability.

Then Satan entered Judas, called Iscariot, one of the Twelve. And Judas went to the chief priests and the officers of the temple guard and discussed with them how he might betray Jesus. They were delighted and agreed to give him money. He consented, and watched for an opportunity to hand Jesus over to them when no crowd was present. Luke 22:3–5

We may be tempted to think that Judas only made a bad decision, but it is clear in Scripture that the thought which resulted in action came from Satan (Anderson, The Bondage Breaker, Chapter 7, pgs. 111–124). The expression "then entered Satan into Judas" is a strong one and definitely shows that, in the opinion of the compilers of the Gospels, there was a person, namely Satan, who bore rule over the powers of evil. It has been suggested as an explanation of the betrayal, which Judas seemed to have believed that he could force the manifestation of Christ's power by placing him in the hands of his enemies. But the acceptance of a reward, miserable though it was, seems to point to greed, and the idea of making friends with the dominant political party, as possible motives of the betrayal. Satan assumed that Jesus' death would end Jesus' mission and thwart God's plan (*Life Application Bible,* pg. 1853).

"Simon, Simon, Satan has asked to sift you as wheat. But I have prayed for you, Simon, that your faith may not fail. And when you have turned back, strengthen your brothers." **Luke 22:31–32**

Peter might not be surprised to hear Jesus say, "The Father and I have been talking about you." Instead, imagine Peter's confusion when he hears Jesus tell him that He and Satan have been talking about him.

The pronoun used here in Greek is the plural you. He is speaking to all the disciples. Satan wants to test all he encounters. If we are ignorant of Satan's schemes, we will be left vulnerable. We need to seek refuge in the Word and in the fellowship of other believers. As Christians, we need a positive attitude about testing. In the book of James, it says we should rejoice when we are tempted because the testing of our faith produces endurance

(James 1:2–3). The scripture teaches that if we confess our sins, God is faithful to forgive us our sins, and to cleanse us from all unrighteousness, because the blood of Jesus cleanses us from all sins (1 John 1:7, 9). (*Standard Lesson Commentary*, pg. 187)

Satan asked permission to "sift" Peter and Jesus allowed it. Through this "sifting," He knew they would be refined. Satan's intention was to find chafe only and to blow it away, but Jesus knew that when Peter saw how much chafe was in him, he would repent and then become more effective in ministering to others. Satan meant the sifting for evil, but God meant it for good. (Hammond, *Demons and Deliverance,* pg. 136)

This saying of Jesus is a mysterious one; it shows something of what is going on in the unseen world. Jesus addressed Peter reminding him that rock like strength is not to be found in self-confidence. Jesus assured Peter that his faith would falter but not be destroyed. In the Lord's prayer the disciples were taught to pray "to deliver us from evil, or the evil one." Satan believes us unworthy and believes he can lure us away with his lies. However, we are washed by the blood of the lamb and are made worthy. Jesus says He prayed for Simon, therefore the request from Satan apparently was not refused. Simon fell, but the result of the fall was not disastrous, but bitter remorse and repentance.

There is a major contrast between accusation and conviction. This is shown between Judas and Peter. Judas betrayed Jesus for thirty pieces of silver. When he realized what he had done he gave in to the accusations of Satan and gave in to sorrow and hung himself. Was his suicide the result of the accusation of Satan or of the conviction of God? Accusations leads to death; conviction leads to repentance and life. Peter also failed Jesus by denying Him. The remorse that Peter felt had to be as painful as that of Judas because he had so clearly promised that he would never run, but stand with Jesus. However, the difference between these two disciples is Peter's sorrow was from conviction which led to repentance. (Anderson, *The Bondage Breaker,* Chapter 5, pgs. 75–94)

———————————

> *Then Peter said, "Ananias, how is it that Satan has so filled your heart that you have lied to the Holy Spirit and have kept for yourself some of the money you received for the land? Didn't it belong to you before it was sold? And after it was sold, wasn't the money at your disposal? What made you think of doing such a thing? You have not lied to men but to God . . ." Peter said to her, "How could you agree to test the Spirit of the Lord? Look! The feet of the men who buried your husband are at the door, and they will carry you out also."* **Acts 5:3–5, 9**

We are responsible for our own actions and attitudes. Satan only takes advantage of the opportunities we give him. If we continually give him access he will assume squatters rights. We don't loose our salvation but we will loose our daily victory and joy in Christ. (Anderson, *The Bondage Breaker,* Chapter 8, pgs. 125–140)

Although we are filled with the Holy Spirit, we are not immune to Satan's temptations. The sin here is not selling the land, but lying to God and God's people. Dishonesty, greed, and covetousness are destructive in a church, preventing the Holy Spirit from working effectively. When we lie to God and God's people, we destroy our testimony for Christ.

———————————

Then I asked, "Who are you Lord?" "I am Jesus, whom you are persecuting," the Lord replied. "Now get up and stand on your feet. I have appeared to you to appoint you as a servant and as a witness of what you have seen of me and what I will show you. I will rescue you from your own people and from the Gentiles. I am sending you to them to open their eyes and turn them from darkness to light, and from the power of Satan to God, so that they may receive forgiveness of sins and a place among those who are sanctified by faith in me." **Acts 26:15–18**

Everyone makes mistakes, and most of us at some time make big mistakes. We make mistakes in relationships, personal behavior, finances, and in religious decisions or activities. Jesus died and rose from the dead. This victory over Satan makes it possible for us to be freed from the snares he puts in our paths. Remember the world is being deceived by Satan, and if we look at the lost as enemies, we will not be motivated to confront Satan to rescue them (*Standard Lesson Commentary*, pg. 203).

God is sending Paul to the Gentiles. They are now to have an equal share in God's inheritance. This inheritance is laid out in 1 Peter 1:3–5.

The God of peace will soon crush Satan under your feet.
Romans 16:20

Christians should study the Word themselves; they will not be fooled. Always compare what you hear with what the scriptures say. It is this knowledge and spiritual wisdom that defeats or "crushes" Satan. He cannot lie to those who study and search the scriptures for themselves.

The husband should fulfill his marital duty to his wife, and likewise the wife to her husband. The wife's body does not belong to her alone but also to her husband. In the same way, the husband's body does not belong to him alone but also to his wife. Do not deprive each other except by mutual consent and for a time, so that you may devote yourself to prayer. Then come together again so that Satan will not tempt you because of your lack of self-control. **I Corinthians 7:3–5**

All physical, emotional and sexual temptations can be difficult to withstand because of our natural desires that God has given us. All of these desires are gifts from God, even sexuality. One is not better than the other. However, Satan tries to use the mental and physical passions of the body to lure us toward him.

For we wanted to come to you, certainly I, Paul, did, again and again, but Satan stopped us.
I Thessalonians 2:18

We do not know what exactly kept Paul away, only that Satan was blocking his arrival. We need to remember that many of the difficulties that prevent us from accomplishing God's work can be attributed to Satan.

Concerning the coming of our Lord Jesus Christ and our being gathered to him, we ask you, brothers, not to become easily unsettled or alarmed by some prophesy, report or letter supposed to have come from us, saying that the day of the Lord has already come. Don't let anyone deceive you in any way, for that day will not come, until the rebellion occurs and the man of lawlessness is revealed, the man doomed to destruction. He will oppose and will exalt himself over everything that is called God or is worshipped, so that he sets himself up in God's temple, proclaiming himself to be God. Don't you remember that when I was with you I used to tell you these things? And now you know what is holding him back, so that he may be revealed at the proper time. For the secret power of lawlessness is already at work; but the one who now holds it back will continue to do so till he is taken out of the way. And then the lawless one will be revealed whom the Lord Jesus will overthrow with the breath of his mouth and destroy by the splendor of his coming. The coming of the lawless one will be in accordance with the work of Satan displayed in all kinds of counterfeit miracles, signs and wonders, and in every sort of evil that deceives those who are perishing. They perish because they refused to love the truth and so be saved. For this reason, God sends them a powerful delusion so that they will believe the lie and so that all will be condemned who have not believed the truth but have delighted in wickedness.

2 Thessalonians 2:1–12

There are various views as to the identity of the restraining influence. It seems evident that it is the Holy Spirit. In Genesis 6:3, the Holy Spirit acts as a restrainer of inequity. It is used in the same way in John concerning the coming of the Holy Spirit. In the New Testament, however, an indwelling of the Holy Spirit is received by the believer, not just in temporary assistance but a permanent indwelling.

The man of sin will be revealed when the restrainer is "taken out of the way." This will be when the church is translated and the Spirit's restraining ministry through it will cease. Notice, however, that it is not said that the restrainer will be "taken away," but "taken out of the way," thus the Holy Spirit will continue a divine activity to the end time though not as a restrainer of evil through the church. (*New Scofield Bible,* pg. 1694)

Throughout history there have been those who are the epitome of evil. They have lived in every generation and will continue to work their evil. The "lawless man" will be **the** Antichrist. We need to be ready for anything that threatens our faith. If our faith is strong, we need not be afraid. How do we discern miracles from God and miracles from Satan? Miracles from God strengthen our faith and lead people to Christ (*Living Application Bible,* pg. 2182). Look at the purpose behind the miracles–does it point to God and His glory or is the purpose to lead people away. Remember: Satan can do miracles, but his purpose is to deceive.

But even when the archangel Michael, when he was disputing with the devil about the body of Moses, did not dare to bring a slanderous accusation against him, but said, "The Lord rebuke you!" **Jude 1:9**

This quote probably comes from a non-canonical book called "The Assumption of Moses" (*Life Application Bible,* pg. 2293). The devil claimed the body of Moses on the grounds that he was a murderer. This was blasphemy, which Michael could not tolerate, yet he did not charge the devil with blasphemy, but simply said,

"The Lord rebuke thee." Notice that we do not have the power to rebuke Satan on our own but God does. Therefore, we can rebuke Satan in the Lord's name or have God do the rebuking for us.

"I know your afflictions and your poverty, yet you are rich! I know the slander of those who say they are Jews and are not, but are a synagogue of Satan. Do not be afraid of what you are about to suffer. I tell you, the devil will put some of you in prison to test you, and you will suffer persecution for ten days. Be faithful, even to the point of death, and I will give you the crown of life."
Revelation 2:9–10

Persecution comes from Satan not God. Satan may harm our physical bodies but he cannot harm our spiritual selves. Pain is part of life. If we experience difficult times, we must not let that turn us away from God. Instead let it draw us toward greater faithfulness (*Life Application Bible*, pg. 2302). There is room for differences of opinion among Christians in some areas, but there is no room for heresy and moral impunity. Do not tolerate sin by bowing to the pressure of open-mindedness.

"I will make those of the synagogue of Satan, who claim to be Jews though they are not, but are liars, I will make them come and fall down at your feet and acknowledge that I have loved you. Since you have kept my command to endure patiently, I will also keep you from the hour of

trial that is going to come upon the whole world to test those who live on the earth." **Revelation 3:9–10**

"I will also keep you from the hour of trial" could mean a time of tribulation in which believers will be spared, or that believers will go through it like everyone else but God will strengthen them in the midst of it, or great distress throughout the ages. Whatever the case, the emphasis should be patiently obeying God no matter what we face.

"To the angel of the church in Laodicea write: These are the words of the Amen, the faithful and true witness, the ruler of God's creation. I know your deeds, that you are neither cold nor hot. I wish you were either one or the other! So, because you are lukewarm–neither hot nor cold–I am about to spit you out of my mouth."You say, 'I am rich; I have acquired wealth and do not need a thing.' But you do not realize that you are wretched, pitiful, poor, blind and naked. I counsel you to buy from me gold refined in the fire, so you can become rich; and white clothes to wear, so you can cover your shameful nakedness; and salve to put on your eyes, so you can see. Those whom I love I rebuke and discipline. So be earnest, and repent. **Revelation 3:14–19**

God will discipline lukewarm people and churches. His purpose in discipline is to bring people back to Him. Satan wants us lukewarm. How do we stop him? Draw near to God through confession, service, worship, and studying the Word, prayer, asking the Holy Spirit to re-ignite our zeal for God and allow Him to work in our hearts.

The rest of mankind that were not killed by these plagues still did not repent of the work of their hands; they did not stop worshipping demons, and idols of gold, silver, bronze, stone and wood, idols that cannot see or hear or walk. Nor did they repent of their murders, their magic arts, their sexual immorality or their thefts.
Revelation 9:20–21

Sin is insidious and takes over our life slowly; in little steps and little bites. It is so gradual we hardly realize it is happening. Temptation entertained today becomes tomorrow's sins. Always stay actively conscious of your need to confess and repent of your sins before God.

False Teachers/Apostles/Messengers

There are many ways in which Satan, "the god of this world," seeks to deceive us. Just as he did with Eve, the devil tries to convince us to rely on ourselves and to try to get our needs met through the world around us, rather than trusting in the provision of our Father in heaven. It is important to know that in addition to being deceived by the world, false teachers, and deceiving sprits, we can also deceive ourselves. (Anderson, *Winning Spiritual Warfare*, pg. 25)

Since we acknowledge that Satan is real and his demons are real, we must then ask how these demons are organized. Who gives the orders and who obeys them? Remember that Satan is in charge. Under him range a large and horrendous crew of demons and creatures bent on destruction. (Masello, *Fallen Angels*, pg. 23)

> *Then they understood that he was not telling them to guard against the yeast used in bread, but against the teaching of the Pharisees and Sadducees.*
> **Matthew 16:12**

Just a small amount of evil can affect a large group of people. Wrong teachings lead people astray. Beware of saying this little sin can't really effect anyone, that is what Satan wants us to believe.

For such men are false apostles, deceitful workmen, masquerading as apostles of Christ. And no wonder, for Satan himself masquerades as an angel of light. It is not surprising, then, if his servants masquerade as servants of righteousness. Their end will be what their actions deserve. **2 Corinthians 11:13–15**

Satan's typical devices are to deceive, to masquerade as an angel of light. Satan and his servants can deceive us by appearing to be good and moral. Don't be fooled by external appearances. Don't be lead astray by Bible quoting speakers. Does the teaching confirm Scripture, and proclaim that Jesus Christ is God who came into the world to save us from sin? If that is not what you are hearing—-run.

It is not raving demoniacs, who are causing the church to be ineffective, but Satan's subtle deception and intrusion into the lives of believers. Satan is a deceiver. The truth of God's Word exposes him and his lies. Just as a cockroach runs to shadows when the lights are turned on, Satan runs for the shadows when the light of God's Word is declared. Believe, declare and act upon the truth of God's Word and you will have victory in Christ. (Anderson, *The Bondage Breaker*, Chapter 10, pgs. 153–170)

To keep me from becoming conceited because of these surpassingly great revelations, there was given me a thorn in my flesh, a messenger of Satan, to torment me. Three times I pleaded with the Lord to take it away from me. But he said to me, "My grace is sufficient for you, for my power is made perfect in weakness." Therefore I will boast all the more gladly about my weakness, so that

Christ's power may rest on me. That is why, for Christ's sake, I delight in weakness, in insults, in hardships, in persecutions, in difficulties. For when I am weak, then I am strong. **2 Corinthians 12:7–10**

The saints, and the martyrs, overcame Satan because they had been washed free of sin by the blood of the Lamb of God. Christ atoned for all sins on the cross of Calvary. The saints overcame Satan by giving their own personal testimonies. The most powerful words that one can ever speak on behalf of Jesus are those of personal testimony. Through testimony, a person tells others what Jesus has meant in his/her personal life. (Rogerson, *The Angels of God*, handout).

Like Paul, Satan has given some of our bothers and sisters thorns in their flesh. The fact that God's power is displayed in weak people should give us courage. We should recognize our limitations, and seek God to open pathways for effective ministry. We need to remember to rely on God for our effectiveness. In admitting our weaknesses, we affirm God's strength. When we are weak, ask God to fill us with His power.

The Spirit clearly says that in later times some will abandon the faith and follow deceiving spirits and things taught by demons. **1 Timothy 4:1**

Satan works in two ways, overt and covert. Here the overt activity is seducing. The word seducing in Greek is defined as "to take you by the hand and lead you so slowly off tract that you don't even realize you're going off track" (Renner, *Seducing Spirits and Doctrine of Demons*, pg. 60). The person whom the seducing spirit is working through is deceived also. They believe they are headed in the right direction.

False doctrines are not about devils, but emanate from devils. Demonic spirits stand against the Holy Spirit and the mystery of godliness to mislead and whisper their false teachings in any way possible.

False teachers will be a threat to the church until the Second Coming of Christ. If false teachers are left unchecked, they will distort the Christian faith. If the words contradict the Bible, they are false; if it causes division and dilutes faith it is false. Remember these false teachings can be extremely subtle.

But there were also false prophets among the people, just as there will be false teachers among you. They will secretly introduce destructive heresies, even denying the sovereign Lord who bought them—bringing swift destruction on themselves. Many will follow their shameful ways and will bring the way of truth into disrepute. In their greed these teachers will exploit you with stories they have made up. Their condemnation has long been hanging over them, and their destruction has not been sleeping. For if God did not spare angels when they sinned, but sent them to hell, putting them into gloomy dungeons to be held for judgment; to be held for judgment; if he did not spare the ancient world when he brought the flood on its ungodly people, but protected Noah, a preacher of righteousness, and seven others; if he condemned the cities of Sodom and Gomorrah, by burning them to ashes, and made them an example of what is going to happen to the ungodly; and if he rescued Lot, a righteous man, who was distressed by the filthy lives of lawless men (for that righteous man, living among them day after day, was tormented in his righteous soul by the lawless deeds he saw and heard)—if this is so, then the Lord knows how to rescue godly men from trials and to hold the unrighteous for the day of judgment, while continuing their punishment. This is especially true of those who follow the corrupt desire of the sinful nature and despite authority. Bold and arrogant, these men are not afraid to slander celestial beings; yet even angels, although they are stronger and more powerful, do not bring slanderous accusations against such beings in the presence of the Lord. But these men blaspheme in matters they do not understand. They are like brute beasts, creatures of instinct, born only to be caught and destroyed, and like beasts they too will perish. They will be paid back with harm for the harm they have done. Their idea of pleasure is to carouse in broad daylight. They are blots and blemishes, reveling in their pleasures while they feast with you. With eyes full of adultery, they never stop sinning; they seduce the unstable; they are experts in greed—an accursed brood! They have left the straight way and wandered off to follow the way of Balaam, son of Beor, who loved the wages of wickedness. But he was rebuked for his wrongdoing by a donkey—a beast without speech—who spoke with a man's voice and restrained the prophet's madness. These men are springs without water and mists driven by a storm. Blackest darkness is reserved for them. For they mouth empty, boastful words and by appealing to the lustful desires of sinful human nature, they entice people who are just escaping from those who live in error. They promise them freedom, while they themselves are slaves of depravity—for a man is a slave to whatever has mastered him. **2 Peter 2:1–19**

False teachers can twist the teachings of Christ. If God did not spare the angels that sinned, he surely will not spare the ungodly and false teachers, preachers and prophets.

In the light of this scripture, the underlying theme of witch-craft is revealed. The author's warning to Timothy also notes the nature of the covert workings of Satan. That deadly, hidden work is the production of a "doctrine of demons." A doctrine is a state-ment of belief. The use of the word doctrine implies a satanic system of belief that appears to be appealing, worst of all true. We need to remember that the cleverest liar makes statements that sound nearly like truth. Many Christians, though saved by believ-ing the truth, have been rendered spiritually impotent through accepting, along with the truth, a doctrine of Satan. It is through knowing the truth of Scripture that we can resist Satan's subver-sions. Subversion means "less than the truth." (Renner, *Seducing Spirits and Doctrine of Demons*, pg. 11)

Now I say to the rest of you in Thyatira, to you who do not hold to her teaching and have not learned Satan's so called deep secrets (I will not impose any other burden on you), **Revelations 2:24**

"Deep secrets" of Satan can be false teaching or secret insights by so called believers "guaranteed" to promote deeper spiritual insight. We need to view with caution new teachings that turn us away from the Bible, fellowship of the church and our basic confessions of faith (*Life Application Bible*, pg. 2304).

Demons And Fallen Angels

The Greek *diamonia* is translated "demons" never devils. There is only one *diabolos* or devil. The New Testament Scriptures hear abundant testimony to the reality and personality of demons. Demons are spirits; Satan's emissaries are so numerous as to make Satan's power practically ubiquitous. They are capable of entering and controlling both humans and animals, and to earnestly seek embodiment, without which, apparently, they are powerless to do evil.

Demon influence and demon possession are distinguished in the New Testament. Demons are unclean, sullen, violent, and malicious. They know Jesus Christ as Most High God and recognize His supreme authority. They know their eternal fate to be one of torment. They inflict physical maladies. Mental disease is to be distinguished from the disorder of mind due to demonic control. Demon influence may manifest itself in religious asceticism (A person who practices extreme self-denial, self-mortification or self-mutilation for religious reasons); degenerating into uncleanness.

The sign of demon influence in religion is departure from the faith. The demons maintain a conflict with Christians who would be spiritual. The Christian's resources are prayer and bodily control, "The full armor of God." All unbelievers are open to demon possession. One of the awful features of the apocalyptic judgments in which this age will end is an emergence of demons out of the abyss. (*New Schofield Bible*, pg. 1330)

All believers are under attack from Satan's forces. We are a target for him to oppose, hinder, hurt, and destroy if at all possible.

From outside of our person, these powers can draw very near to inject their temptations into our minds, to tamper without emotions, to soften and condition our wills, and to assault our bodies. It takes an all out application of our spiritual resources to stand strong against this oppressive assault.

> *When men began to increase in number on the earth and daughters were born to them, the sons of God saw that the daughters of men were beautiful, and they married any of them they chose. Then the LORD said, "My Spirit will not contend with man forever for he is mortal; his days will be a hundred and twenty years. The Nephilim were on the earth in those days, and also afterward, when the sons of God went to the daughters of men and had children by them. They were the heroes of old, men of renown. The LORD saw how great man's wickedness on the earth had become, and that every inclination of the thoughts of his heart was only evil all the time. The LORD was grieved that he had made man on the earth, and his heart was filled with pain.* **Genesis 6:1–6**

"Sons of God" is a title of the higher order of supernatural spiritual beings, which surround God's throne. Elsewhere 'sons of God' refer to angelic beings, good and bad. "Sons of God" are said to be the fallen angels who lusted after daughters of man and entered into abnormal sexual relations. Their punishment was severe. The off spring were called Nephilim in Hebrew (Jeremiah, 72). These Nephilim grieved God by their sin, just as when we sin we grieve God.

"Sons of God" were also called Watchers. In 1 Enoch, a Hebrew book not in our Old Testament, this order of angels known as Watchers, kept a close eye on the affairs of men. Watchers never slept and studied this new order of man, the females of the human race. The watchers not only came down to earth and mated, they also instructed their wives in all sorts of forbidden and arcane arts. (Masello, *Fallen Angels*, pg. 17)

We saw the Nephilim there (descendants of Anak comes from the Nephilim). We seemed like grasshoppers in our own eyes, and we looked the same to them.
Numbers 13:33

Nephilim–giants that lived on earth before the flood. It is a possibility that Goliath was a Nephilim.

The Nephilim were supposedly the children of the angels in Genesis 6. Stitching together the story from Genesis and Enoch, these giants were wiped out by God through Michael who rounded them up and imprisoned them in the valley of the earth, where they joined Satan's army. (Masello, *Fallen Angels*, pg. 18)

When he arrived at the other side in the region of the Gadarenes, two demon-possessed men coming from the tombs met him. They were so violent that no one could pass that way. "What do you want with us, Son of God?" they shouted. "Have you come here to torture us before the appointed time?" Some distance from them a large herd of pigs was feeding. The demons begged Jesus, "If you drive us out, send us into the herd of pigs." He said to then, "Go!" So they came out and went into the pigs, and the whole herd rushed down the steep bank into the

> lake and died in the water. Those tending the pigs ran
> off, went into the town and reported all this including
> what had happened to the demon-possessed men. Then
> the whole town went out to meet Jesus. And when they
> saw him, they pleaded with him to leave their region.
> **Matthew 8:28–34**

The Jewish priests used incantations in dealing with demon-possessed people. They used a root called *baaras*. When used correctly the demon would come out through the nose. Jesus needs no incantation. He only needs a word of command. If demons are the supreme woe, then Jesus is the Master of man's woes.

The evil spirits are aware that retribution awaits them in the future and they are afraid, (Hammond, *Demons and Deliverance*, pg. 19). Those who are knowingly disobedient deprive themselves of divine protection and place themselves at the mercy of the forces of evil. Demons, when confronted by Jesus or the blood of Jesus, loose their power. Demons know Jesus to be the Son of God, belief is not enough; faith is accepting Jesus, repentance, and obeying his commands. Unclean men, gentiles, and the demon-possessed lived in graveyards. Jesus helped anyway. We too must not turn away from those who are tormented. Do we offer them God and even at times pray for their deliverance?

Jesus did not simply go about the earth speaking kind and loving words toward people. He reached out and touched people. He spoke words of love towards people. Talk is cheap. Actions speak louder than words. Through His actions, He confronted human need. Wherever good is served, evil is threatened, and when evil is threatened, evil often responds in violence. When we look at the chains that bind us, whether physical, emotional or spiritual, Jesus wants to set us free and give us abundant life (*Standard Lesson Commentary*, pg. 118).

In His Sermon on the Mount, Jesus made a point of telling His own, "Do not be anxious for your life." Reminding them of the birds and the lilies of the field which He cares for, He assured them He would care for them since they are far more important to Him than birds and flowers (and according to my daughter, pigs). Remember, Satan enjoys it when we get ourselves upset and agitated by worrying. Someone has well remarked that most of what we worry about never comes to pass. One of the devil's tricks is to keep us so busy worrying about things we can do nothing about; we fail to do anything about the things we can change (Lightner, *Angels, Satan, and Demons*, pg. 81).

———————

When the Son of Man comes in his glory, and all the angels with him, he will sit on his throne in heavenly glory. All the nations will be gathered before him, and he will separate the people one from another as a shepherd separates the sheep from the goats. He will put the sheep on his right and the goats on his left. "Then the King will say to those on his right, 'Come, you who are blessed by my Father; take your inheritance, the kingdom prepared for you since the creation of the world. For I was hungry and you gave me something to eat, I was thirsty and you gave me something to drink, I was a stranger and you invited me in, I needed clothes and you clothed me, I was sick and you looked after me, I was in prison and you came to visit me.'" "Then the righteous will answer him, 'Lord, when did we see you hungry and feed you, or thirsty and give you something to drink? When did we see you a stranger and invite you in, or needing clothes and clothe you? When did we see you sick or in prison and go to visit you?"' "The king will reply, 'I tell you the truth, whatever you did for one of the least of these brothers of mine, you did for me.'" "Then he will say to those of his left, 'Depart from me, you who are cursed, into the eternal fire prepared for the devil and his angels.'" **Matthew 25:31–41**

God will come in judgment of Satan and his demons. Even demons have a home, and Hell was the one that God had chosen for them. The "who" of the demons and Satan are not the most important issue in this scripture but the "what." Satan and his demons will be sent to the eternal fire. This scripture gives us a taste of that place, while describing how Jesus, on Judgment Day, will go about separating the good from the wicked.

Calling the twelve to him, he sent them out two by two and gave them authority over evil spirits. **Mark 6:7**

He sent them "two by two" as the law required for verification of testimony of witnesses. This is an example of the idea that God stands above culture, and He desires that we present His message in ways that speak to each culture. Note in Mark 6:13 the disciples had been given the power to continue His mission. Repentance is the first element of their ministry. The second is the exorcism of demons and thirdly, healing. The things Jesus emphasized to His disciples then are still true today, not everyone will respond positively to the message of salvation (*Standard Lesson Commentary*, pg. 257).

The disciples were given power over evil spirits or demons. Christ sent them two by two as a team so they could strengthen each other. We cannot go it alone against the world or against

Satan. All Christians may be reminded of their position in this world as the representatives and ministers of Christ.

The twelve were with him, and also some women who had been cured of evil spirits and diseases: Mary (called Magdalene) from whom seven demons had come out; Joanna the wife of Cuza, the manager of Herod's household; Suzanna: and many others. **Luke 8:2–3b**

Jesus offered women the same healing, joy and service as he did men. He showed all people are equal in God's love and service.

If Satan is divided against himself, how can his kingdom stand? I say this because you claim that I drive out demons by Beelzebub. **Luke 11:18**

Satan cannot divide his own kingdom. The kingdom of God has arrived with the coming of Jesus Christ. Notice the name used for Satan here is Beelzebub.

Jesus is accused of complicity with Beelzebub and was challenged for a sign to clear Him of the charge. He refuses the charge by an appeal to common sense. Jesus overshadowed His victory over Satan. The true explanation of His cures; the power of God was present with Him and the kingdom of God had come among them. He goes on to point out the impossibility of being neutral in the conflict between Himself and Satan.

> *When an evil spirit comes out of a man, it goes through arid places seeking rest and does not find it. Then it says, "I will return to the house I left." When it arrives, it finds the house swept clean and put in order. Then it goes and takes seven other spirits more wicked than itself, and they go in and live there. And the final condition of a man is worse than the first.* **Luke 11:24–26**

Jesus was illustrating an unfortunate human tendency; our desire to reform often does not last long. It is not enough to be emptied of will; we must then be filled with the power of the Holy Spirit to accomplish God's new purpose in our lives. (*Life Application Bible*, pg. 1826)

Demons can only find rest in physical beings, preferring even swine over nothingness. Demons are spiritual entities and are therefore not subject to barriers of the physical world. The walls of a church do not establish it as a sanctuary; only salvation, prayer and spiritual authority given by Christ through the Holy Spirit can do that.

Demons can communicate with each other. They can also communicate with us through a human subject. Each spirit has an identity that is unique. They are not just impersonal forces. The fact that they can leave and then come back shows their ability to think and plan. Notice that the evil spirit found the person he left "swept and put in order." This shows that evil spirits can evaluate their surroundings. They therefore, can evaluate our hearts to gain access to our lives through our points of vulnerability. Demons can combine forces, therefore, making the situation worse.

Verse 26 says that the first demon brought back seven others worse than itself, which shows they vary in degree of wickedness. Remember: if we continue to walk in the light of God's Word, we don't need to be afraid of the spirits of darkness. (Anderson, *The Bondage Breaker*, Chapter 5, pgs. 75–94)

This girl followed Paul and the rest of us, shouting, "These men are servants of the Most High God, who are telling you the way to be saved." **Acts 16:17**

The fortune telling slave persisted in shouting unsolicited testimonials until Paul exorcised the demon. We clearly see that demons know the way to salvation, but knowledge of "how" is not salvation.

The slave girl spoke the truth, although it was from a demon that she received the knowledge. Paul kept separate the truths of God from all demons words. Truth and evil do not mix.

No, but the sacrifice offered to pagans are offered to demons, not to God, and I do not want you to be participants with demons. You cannot drink the cup of the Lord and the cup of demons too; you cannot have a part in both the Lord's table and the table of demons.
1 Corinthians 10:20–21

We share in the symbolic blood of Christ in the Lord's Table. Are there places in our lives that we try to participate as Christians and pagan? Is Christ first in our lives?

"In your anger do not sin." Do not let the sun go down while you are still angry, and do not give the devil a foothold.
Ephesians 4:26–27 or 2 Corinthians 2:10–11

The Bible doesn't tell us that we shouldn't feel angry, but it points out that it is important to handle our anger properly. If vented thoughtlessly, anger can hurt others and destroy relationships. If bottled up inside, it can cause us to become bitter and destroy us from within. Deal with anger immediately in such a way as to build up relationships. If we nurse our anger, we will give Satan an opportunity to divide us. Don't let any day end before we begin to work on mending relationships.

The word "foothold" literally means "place." Paul is saying we could possibly allow the devil a place in our lives if we fail to speak the truth in love and attempt emotional honesty. Anger can turn to bitterness and a refusal or inability to forgive which opens us up to demonic attack.

You believe that there is one God. Good! Even the demons believe that, and shudder. **James 2:19**

There are those who recite the articles of faith, but merely reciting the beliefs without any resulting deeds does not bring salvation. Demons give assent and their belief is clearly worthless and they tremble, as they contemplate meeting God in judgment. Mere intellectual belief is not the faith that saves. Remember that Satan and demons know God, as we cannot. They were His Holy angels thrown from heaven.

And the angels who did not keep their positions of authority but abandoned their own home, these he has kept in darkness, bound with everlasting chains for judgment on the great Day. In a similar way, Sodom and Gomorrah and the surrounding towns gave themselves up to sexual immorality and perversion. They serve as an example of those who suffer the punishment of eternal fire. In the very same way, these dreamers pollute their own bodies, reject authority and slander celestial beings.
Jude 1:6–8

The evil characteristics underlined throughout are sensual indulgences and a spirit of self-willed rebelliousness. Calling men dreamers may point to the way in which they conjure up fantasies and imaginings that are of an impure kind. These evil imaginings and fantasies do not remain in their minds and hearts but are translated into action. They "defile the flesh" implies that the flesh itself is not impure but is defiled by misuse.

The angels, once pure and holy and living in God's presence, gave in to pride and followed Satan to rebel against God. "Celestial beings" are probably angels. False teachers slander the realities of the spiritual world. Either they don't believe in Satan, or they take Satan's power lightly. Many in our world today mock the supernatural. Do not take Satan or evil lightly. He is at work now trying to render Christians complacent and ineffective. Through prayer we can rebuke Satan and bind him through the power of Jesus.

The Antichrist/The Beast/The Dragon

Many identify the "beast coming up out of the earth" as the Anti-christ. According to Scripture "many antichrists" and those who have the "spirit of the antichrist" precede and prepare the way for the final Antichrist. The supreme mark of all antichrists is the denial of the incarnation of the eternal Son of God. If the "beast coming up out of the earth" is the Anti-Christ, he is the same as the "false prophet." Because the word Antichrist is never directly applied to him, however, some consider the term anti-christ, defined in the sense against Christ, as applying to the first beast, who is the political ruler.

Dear children, this is the last hour; and as you have heard that the antichrist is coming, even now many antichrists have come. This is how we know it is the last hour. They went out from us, but they did not really belong to us. For if they had belonged to us, they would have remained with us; but their going showed that none of them belonged to us. But you have an anointing from the Holy One, and all of you know the truth. I do not write to you because you do not know the truth, but because you do know it and because no lie comes from the truth. Who is the liar? It is the man who denies that Jesus is the Christ. Such a man is the antichrist—he denies the Father and the Son. No one who denies the Son has the Father; whoever acknowledges the Son has the Father also. See that what you have heard from the beginning remains in you. If it does, you also will remain in the Son and in the Father.

And this is what he promised us—even eternal life. I am writing these things to you about those who are trying to lead you astray. As for you, the anointing you received from him remains in you, and you do not need anyone to teach you. But as his anointing teaches you about these things and as that anointing is real, not counterfeit—just as it has taught you, remain in him. **1 John 2:18–27**

We are charged to teach God's word clearly and carefully to the new members and weaker members so they won't fall prey to these teachers who come as wolves in sheep's clothing. Be aware there are those in our fellowship for reasons other than Christ, perhaps tradition, social or business contact opportunities, or habit. We can assist those to become personally acquainted with Jesus Christ. When we are lead by the Spirit, we can stand against all things. Ask for guidance each day.

Then another sign appeared in heaven: an enormous red dragon with seven heads and ten horns and seven crowns of his heads. His tail swept a third of the stars our of the sky and flung them to the earth. The dragon stood in front of the woman who was about to give birth, so that he might devour her child the moment it was born. She gave birth to a son, a male child, who will rule all the nations with an iron scepter. And her child was snatched up to God and to his throne. The woman fled into the desert to a place prepared for her by God, where she might be taken care of for 1,260 days. And there was war in heaven. Michael and his angels fought against the dragon, and the dragon and his angels fought back.

> *But he was not strong enough, and they lost their place in heaven. The great dragon was hurled down—that ancient serpent, called the devil, or Satan, who leads the whole world astray. He was hurled to the earth, and his angels with him.* **Revelation 12:3–9**

The dragon is shown to be the Antichrist of the spiritual world, just as the beast is the earthly Antichrist sharing his characteristics. They are shown to retain one horrible concentration of evil.

The desert represents spiritual refuge and protection from Satan. God aided the woman and we can be sure He offers security to all believers. Satan always attacks God's people, but God keeps us spiritually secure. We must remember that Christ is victorious, because of Christ's death on the cross. Satan is not a symbol or a legend. He is very real. Originally, Satan was an angel of God, but through his own pride and sin was thrown out of heaven and God's presence. The devil is God's enemy, and he constantly tries to hinder God's work, but is limited by God (*Life Application Bible*, pg. 2318). God is still in control. Jesus has complete power over Satan.

> *And the dragon stood on the shore of the sea. And I saw a beast coming out of the sea. He had ten horns and seven heads with ten crowns on his horns, and on each head a blasphemous name. The beast I saw resembled a leopard, but had feet like those of a bear and a mouth like that of a lion. The dragon gave the beast his power and his throne and great authority. One of the heads of the beast seemed to have had a fatal wound, but the fatal wound had been*

healed. The whole world was astonished and followed the beast. **Revelation 13:1–3**

In this unveiling of conditions on the earth at the end of the age, the following factors will be manifest: The world ruler is satanically energized; he and his image will be worshipped; he is acknowledged as possessing supreme military power; he exercises a universal authority and he persecutes the believers in Christ. The second beast is a deceiver and he exercises economic dictatorship. The fourth beast is the ten kings. The whole vision is the last form of world power, a confederation of ten nations which will be a revival of the old Roman Empire.

The woman arrayed in purple and scarlet is seen sitting on a scarlet beast. Because the woman rides the beast, where one goes the other goes also; thus the world empire will embrace all the areas of Christendom. Fragments of the ancient Roman Empire have never ceased to exist as separate kingdoms. It was the empirical form of government which ceased; the one head has a "fatal wound." What is written prophetically in verse 3 is the restoration of the empirical form as such, though over a federated empire of ten kingdoms. The head is "healed" restored, and there is an emperor again, the beast.

In the sense of the present world system, the ethically bad sense of the word *world*, refers to the order or arrangement under which Satan has organized the world of unbelieving mankind upon his cosmic principle of force, greed, selfishness, ambition, and pleasure. This world system is imposing and powerful with military might; is often outwardly religious, scientific, cultured, and elegant; but, seething with national and commercial rivalries and ambitions, is upheld in any real crisis only by armed force, and is dominated by satanic principles. (*New Scofield Bible*, pg. 1786)

The beast symbolizes THE Antichrist—not Satan, but someone under Satan's power and control. Many believe that Satan's evil will culminate in a final Antichrist, one who will focus all the powers of evil against Jesus Christ and his followers. Satan and his two evil accomplices form an unholy trinity. To the beast out of the sea, he gave political power. To the beast out of the earth he gave power to do miracles (*Life Application Bible*, pg. 2329). Don't be misled by claims of great miracles, or other acts. When Christ returns he will reveal himself and no one will miss the truth.

Then I saw the beast and the kings of the earth and their armies gathered together to make war against the rider on the horse and his army. But the beast was captured, and with him the false prophet who had performed the miraculous signs on his behalf. With these signs he had deluded those who had received the mark of the beast and worshiped his image. The two of them were thrown alive into the fiery lake of burning sulfur. The rest of them were killed with the sword that came out of the mouth of the rider on the horse, and all the birds gorged themselves on their flesh. **Revelation 19:19–21**

The day of the LORD is that period of time when God openly intervenes in the affairs of men in judgment and in blessing. It will begin with the translation of the church and will terminate with the cleansing of the heavens and the earth before bringing into being the new heavens and the new earth.

The order of events appears to be; the rapture of the church just preceding the beginning of the Day of the LORD; the fulfillment of Daniel's seventieth week (Daniel 9:27), the latter half of which is the great tribulation; the return of the Lord in glory to establish the millennial kingdom; the destruction of the beast, the false prophet, and their armies, which is the "great and awesome" aspect of the day; the judgment of individuals according to their treatment of Christ's brethren; the millennial reign of Christ on earth; the satanic revolt and its judgment; the resurrection and the final judgment of the wicked; the destruction of the present earth and heaven by fire in preparation for the future "Day of God." Finally, the creation of the new heavens and the new earth.

The Beast is earth's last and most awful tyrant, Satan's cruel instrument of wrath and hatred against God and the saints. To the beast, Satan gives the powers which he offered to Christ. (*New Scofield Bible*, pg. 1796)

The battle lines are drawn, the battle begun. There really is no fight because the victory was won when Jesus died on the cross and rose from the dead. The fiery lake of burning sulfur is the final destination of the wicked. This lake is different from the abyss (bottomless pit). The Antichrist, the false prophet, and then Satan himself will be thrown into that lake. Afterward, everyone whose name is not recorded in the book of life will be thrown into the lake of fire (*Life Application Bible*, pg. 2330).

And I saw an angel coming down out of heaven, having the key to the Abyss and holding in his hand a great chain. He seized the dragon, that ancient serpent, who is the devil, or Satan, and bound him for a thousand years. He threw him into the Abyss, and locked and sealed it over him, to keep him from deceiving the nations anymore until the thousand years were ended. After that, he must be set free for a short time. I saw thrones on which were seated those who had been given authority to judge. And I saw the souls of those who had been beheaded because of their testimony for Jesus and because of the word of God. They had not worshiped the beast or his image and had not received his mark on their foreheads or their hands. They came to life and reigned with Christ a thousand years. (The rest of the dead did not come to life until the thousand years were ended.) This is the first resurrection. Blessed and holy are those who have part in the first resurrection. The second death has no power over them, but they will be priests of God and of Christ and will reign with him for a thousand years. When the thousand years are over, Satan will be released from his prison and will go out to deceive the nations in the four corners of the earth, Gog and Magog, to gather them for battle. In number they are like the sand on the seashore. They marched across the breadth of the earth and surrounded the camp of God's people, the city he loves. But fire came down from heaven and devoured them. And the devil, who deceived them, was thrown into the lake of burning sulfur, where the beast and the false prophet had been thrown. They will be tormented day and night for ever and ever. **Revelation 20:1–10**

The expression "thousand years," which occurs six times in verses 1–7, gives rise to the term "Millennium" which comes from the Latin *mill* meaning thousand, and *annus* meaning years. The millennium is that period of time during which Christ will reign upon the earth, a time of universal peace, prosperity, long life, and prevailing righteousness. The early church Fathers interpreted this passage referring to a future literal period of time.

The Seventh Dispensation: the kingdom is the last of the

ordered ages which conditions human life on earth. It is the kingdom covenanted to David. David's greater Son, the Lord Jesus Christ, will rule over the earth as King of kings and Lord of lords for 1000 years, associating with Himself in that reign with His saints of all ages.

The Kingdom Age gathers into itself under Christ the various "times" spoken of in the Scriptures. The time of oppression and misrule ends when Christ establishes His kingdom. The time of testimony and divine forbearance ends in judgment. The time of toil ends in rest and reward. The time of suffering ends in glory. The time of Israel's blindness and chastisement ends in restoration and conversion. The times of the Gentiles end in the smiting of the image and the setting up of the kingdom of heaven. And the time of creation's bondage ends in deliverance at the manifestation of the sons of God.

At the conclusion of the thousand years, Satan is released for a little season and instigates a final rebellion which is summarily put down by the Lord. Christ casts Satan into the Lake of fire to be eternally tormented, defeats the last enemy, death, and then delivers up the kingdom to the Father.

The first resurrection is the resurrection of the just. Although it is shown in both the Old and New Testament that the resurrection of the just to life eternal, and the resurrection of the lost to everlasting condemnation. The two resurrections are a distinction, one from another. This is the first time the precise interval between the two resurrections is revealed as a period of a thousand years. (*New Scofield Bible*, pg. 1796)

There are different views about these thousand years, but they need not cause confusion and controversy. What is most crucial is that Christ will return, defeat Satan and reign forever. Satan's power is not eternal; he will meet his doom (*Life Application Bible*, pg. 2304).

Occult/Names And Groups

More and more people in our world are becoming actively interested in the occult world. They desire to be taken over by spirit powers that they might conduct séances, pronounce curses, become a witch, or secure some other supernatural condition . . . others desire those so called good spirits who will enable them to do white magic or beneficial supernatural deeds that they claim will be for the good of mankind. It all comes from the same deceiver, however, whether it is white or black magic and it results in bondage to Satan.

We must be careful that idle curiosity to look into these subjects does not in itself give Satan an advantage against us.

In today's world, the occult is not always frowned upon. It is either considered a game or not dangerous. The following list is not all-inclusive and some of the items on the list seem harmless, but care must be taken with anything that takes our focus away from Christ.

Witchcraft, spiritualism, reincarnation, fortune telling, mediums, ESP, Eastern Religions, Atlantis, Mu and Lemuria, astrology, and yoga (If centering on Christ is not a major focus and focal point during the exercises. Yoga is big on the college campuses. Participants need to use Christ as the focal point during meditation) voodoo, obeah, Satanism, black magic, parapsychology, meditation (again when focus is empty and not on God) tarot cards, mysticism, demonology, spirit photography, dream interpretation, hypnotism, numerology, I Ching, UFO, prophetic messages, poltergeists, alchemy, sorcery, clairvoyance, Kabbala, levitation, metaphysical healing, automatic writing, use of pendulum,

115

theosophy, autosuggestion, séances, scientology, Process Church of the Final Judgment, Ouija Boards, meditation as a way to get acquainted with your familiar spirit or guardian angel (there are people out there who say they can introduce you?????) brujeria (witchdoctor), macumba (a form of spiritualism with deliverance and exorcism offered through incense and meditations).

Tsagalala—in English is "She-who-watches." She was the spiritual leader of the tribe in Washington State. She participated in black magic, curses and blessings. She believed she exalted over the Great Spirit.

Wicca—males who are part of a witchcraft group, wear their hair short except for a small bunch of hair long in the middle of the back (this is different than a mullet, a hair style from the 60's that is short on the sides and long in the back). This looks like a tail descending from the middle of the head not the bottom. The tail is actually called the goat's tail and is a sign of allegiance to Satan. Be aware of the fads going around, youth may think it looks cool, but what is the origin and the meaning? Following some fads can leave you open to Satanic attack. Ask the Holy Spirit to give you guidance before you follow the crowd.

Cabala is a collection of writings first amassed shortly after 70 AD by the rabbis who fled Jerusalem just before it was conquered by Tiberius. The Cabala has been added to and revised over the generations. Today, it is sold among wealthy Jews, and many books about the Cabalistic beliefs are best sellers in those elite societies. Cabalism is a religion of power, spiritual power that is a continuation of the old forms of worship of Baal and Molech which God so severely condemned throughout the Old Testament. It is really a form of Satan worship, but people who get involved with it never use the term Satan. They teach and serve "the Master." Many simply call the Cabala a set of spiritual beliefs or a philosophy, which is deceptive. Followers of Cabalism do not teach their children the Ten Commandments or teaching of the Hebrew Bible except in a perverse form. (Brown, *Unbroken Curses*, pg. 150)

Some of the list above can be harmless and some can be gifts from God, however, it is important that discernment be used as to whether it is a gift from the Holy Spirit.

Magic, witches and sorcerers are not new. Their existence reaches back in time almost to the beginning of time. Magic, specifically, the conjuring of spirits to do one's bidding was a very serious, extraordinarily complicated, and above all, dangerous business. No sorcerer would think to undertake it without a black book, or grimoire at his side. In these grimoires (literally translated, grammar) were contained all the secrets of the black arts, the rules, rituals and prayers that the magician must faithfully perform. If he failed to follow the instructions properly, he could find himself suddenly at the mercy of whatever demon he had summoned from Hell. Demons were not known for their understanding.

The oldest, and the most sought after, of all these grimoires was something known as *The Key of Solomon*. No surprise, according to one legend, it had been written by the devils themselves. It was given to Solomon, King of Israel in the 10th century b.c., and kept hidden under his throne. A powerful magician, Solomon was considered a master of the occult world; it was even said he had harnessed demons to help in the building of the Temple of Jerusalem. The boon came to be called a "key" after the lines of Matthew 16:19, in which Jesus says to Peter, "And I will give unto thee the keys of the kingdom of heaven; and whatsoever thou shalt bind on earth shall be bound in heaven; and whatsoever thou shalt loose on earth shall be loosed in heaven." The book was considered just such a key, an instrument for opening the doors to secret wisdom.

Although references to the key of Solomon can be found as

early as the first century a.d., the oldest edition which still exists today, housed in the British Museum, is a Greek translation from perhaps the twelfth century. Many other editions, usually in French or Latin, were published in the 1700's.

But what does the book contain? In language that is heavily influenced by astrological and cabalistic doctrine, the book sets out, in elaborate detail, all the steps that must be taken to summon spirits and force them to do as asked. It prescribes the fasting and purification rituals that the magician himself must first undergo before even attempting a conjuration. Then it goes on to explain how to choose the proper time and place; the robes, weapons, and pentacles which will be necessary; the incantations, the drawing of the magic circle (within which the magician will be safe), etc. Though the spirits may be summoned for any number of tasks, they were most commonly invoked to uncover and procure the secret treasures of the Earth. (Maselo, *Fallen Angels*, pg. 87)

I have added this information on the sorcerer's books because they are still in existence, and some of lesser value are currently in circulation. Books called white magic can be found in our libraries. They entice us and our youth with the idea that we too can have power and that this power is not evil, just a way to improve ourselves and to "connect" to the power of the world.

> *Pharaoh then summoned wise men and sorcerers and the Egyptian magicians also did the same things by their secret arts: Each one threw down his staff and it became a snake. But Aaron's staff swallowed up their staffs.*
> **Exodus 7:11–12**

Sorcerers, magicians, and witches, how did they do duplicate miracles? Some trickery, illusions and some may have used satanic powers. However, anything they did seemed to make matters worse. Satan tries to set up counterfeits of things divine in order to confuse our minds and make us mistake the false for the true. Let the Word of God inform us. No miracle from God would endorse any message that is contrary to the teaching of God's Word (*Life Application Bible*, pg. 115).

"Do not allow a sorcerer to live. Anyone who has sexual relations with an animal must be put to death. Whoever sacrifices to any god other than the LORD must be destroyed." **Exodus 22:18–20**

We are told or we hear that witchcraft is founded on mere illusion, and regard witches and wizards as just unfortunate persons, laboring under a certain amount of self-deception. It is generally assumed that to hold actual communication with evil spirits, and obtain spiritual powers is impossible. Those who pretend to be witches or wizards must be considered impostors. We are led to believe that witches and wizards are tricksters. Demonology, magic, delusions, and evil spirits themselves are either nonexistent, or regulated to another sphere, and so entirely beyond human concerns. However, the scriptures tell us something different. Their evil spirits are regarded as really existing, and the witch and wizard have access to them.

Sorcery was punishable by death because it was a crime against God. To invoke evil powers violated the first commandment to "have no other gods." Sorcery was rebellion against God and His authority. It was teaming up with Satan. Today we cannot kill sorcerers, but we can avoid them and their work (*Life Application Bible*, pg. 141).

Do not practice divination or sorcery.
Leviticus 19: 26b

*Do not turn to mediums or seek out spirits, for you will be
defiled by them.* **Leviticus 19:31a**

In Hebrew, the word enchantment means to whisper or mutter after having communications with evil. Familiar spirits are
clearly admitted in this scripture. Scripture clearly states that
mediums, spiritists, divination and sorcery defile the person.
Tampering in these occults can leave us open to attacks by Satan.

*The Moabites said to the elders of Midian, "The horde is going to
lick up everything around us, as an ox licks up the grass of the field."
So Balak son of Zippor, who was king of Moab at that time, sent mes-
sengers to summon Balaam son of Beor, who was at Pethor, near the
River, in his native land. Balak said: "A people has come out of Egypt;
they cover the face of the land and have settled next to me. Now come
and put a curse on these people, because they are too powerful for me.
Perhaps then I will be able to defeat them and drive them out of the
country. For I know that those you bless are blessed, and those you curse
are cursed." The elders of Moab and Midian left, taking with them
the fee for divination. When they came to Balaam, they told him what
Balak had said.* **Numbers 22:4-7**

Balaam was a sorcerer. Belief in curses and blessings was common in Old Testament times. The king wanted a curse on Israel
hoping that by magic God would turn against Israel (*Life Applica-*

tion Bible, pg. 252). This story looks at the disaster of maintaining an outward façade of Christianity and having a corrupt inward life. Who and what we are always comes to the surface. God can make us over from within.

When you enter the land the LORD your God is giving you, do not learn to imitate the detestable ways of the nations there. Let no one be found among you who sacrifices his son or daughter in the fire, who practices divination or sorcery, interprets omens, engages in witchcraft, or casts spells, or who is a medium or spiritist or who consults the dead. **Deuteronomy 18:9–11**

God has His agents and so does Satan. The practices of the occult are a mixture of fraud, guesswork and dealing with evil spirits according to Isaiah. There can be no love and communion with God and trafficking with the devil at the same time. What God wants us to know He will teach us through the proper means, i.e. scripture and what He conceals we have no right or need to seek through evil means. The popular superstitions are very seductive. It is not unusual to be curious about the occult, but we must remember and teach that the occult has Satan behind it. The information Satan offers is likely to be distorted or completely false. As a child walks along the darkest road quite contentedly, so long as its hand is in its father's hand, so with equal confidence may we confide in the safe and unerring guidance of the indwelling of the Holy Spirit.

> *For rebellion is like the sin of divination, and arrogance*
> *like the evil of idolatry. Because you have rejected the*
> *word of the LORD, he has rejected you as king.*
> **1 Samuel 15:23**

Rebellion makes us a worshipper of ourselves rather that of God. It ignores the solemn truth that we cannot serve two masters. It sows the moral seed of evil, which when it takes root, can widen the space between God and us. It is very dangerous to begin to compare our wishes and plans to the possible will of God. Rebellion is a sin equal to divination and arrogance likened to the evil of idolatry. Being religious is not enough if we do not act out of devotion and obedience to God.

> *Now Samuel was dead, and all Israel had mourned for*
> *him and buried him in his own town of Ramah. Saul*
> *had expelled the mediums and spiritists from the land.*
> *The Philistines assembled and came and set up camp at*
> *Shunem, while Saul gathered all the Israelites and set*
> *up camp at Gilboa. When Saul saw the Philistine army,*
> *he was afraid; terror filled his heart. He inquired of the*
> *LORD, but the LORD did not answer him by dreams*
> *or Urim or prophets. Saul then said to his attendants,*
> *"Find me a woman who is a medium, so I may go and*
> *inquire of her. "There is one in Endor," they said. So Saul*
> *disguised himself, putting on other clothes, and at night*
> *he and two men went to the woman. "Consult a spirit*
> *for me," he said, "and bring up for me the one I name."*
> *Because you did not obey the LORD or carry out his fierce*
> *wrath against the Amalekites, the LORD has done this*
> *to you today.* **1 Samuel 28:3–8, 18**

The witch of Endor's usual incantations had been fakes, but not to her terror, God sends Samuel to pronounce Saul's doom. We may make a great show of denouncing sin, but if our hearts are not changed, we will return to it. God wants us to turn to Him, to turn to anything or anyone else leads to disaster.

The woman expected contact with a demon, but to her amazement and terror, God actually permitted Samuel to appear to her and give a message of doom to Saul. The text clearly states that it was Samuel. No agent of Satan could have given a message so clearly from the Lord. The passage does not say that the woman "brought up" Samuel from the dead. The incident gives no support to the false contention of spiritists that they can speak with the dead. Mediums do not have access to the dead but communicate with spirits posing as persons who have died; these are lying demons. (*New Scofield Study Bible*, pg. 433)

When Joram saw Jehu he asked, "Have you come in peace, Jehu?" "How can there be peace," Jehu replied, "as long as all the idolatry and witchcraft of your mother Jezebel abound?" **2 Kings 9:22**

The question in this scripture is peace. Peace is rooted and grounded in God and love for Him. True peace comes from God. But remember there is a difference between peace and tribulation in our lives. When we are one with Christ, we have peace, but the devil wants to separate us from God and from the fellowship of Christians so he brings tribulations to our lives. Are there sins in our lives un-repented? We can be assured that the punishment, if it has not come, awaits us.

They sacrificed their sons and daughters in the fire. They practiced divination and sorcery and sold themselves to do evil in the eyes of the LORD, provoking him to anger. **2 Kings 17:17**

Divination means witchcraft and sorcery is consulting with evil spirits. God forbade forms of witchcraft, fortune telling, and magic. They are wrong because they seek power and guidance from others not God, His law, and His word (*Life Application Bible*, pg. 637). These practices demonstrate a lack of faith in God and open doors to demonic influences. Ingratitude toward God is in the foreground. The wicked throw the whole energy of their souls into their sins, their pursuit of pleasure, their service to the world, the devil and the flesh. But how slack handed and half-hearted we are at times as Christians. Is it a wonder that God's cause suffers?

Manasseh was twelve years old when he became king, and he reigned in Jerusalem fifty-five years. His mother's name was Hephzibah. He did evil in the eyes of the LORD, following the detestable practices of the nations the LORD had driven out before the Israelites. He rebuilt the high places his father Hezekiah had destroyed; he also erected altars to Baal and made an Asherah pole, as Ahab king of Israel had done. He bowed down to all the starry hosts and worshipped them. He built altars in the temple of the LORD, of which the LORD had said, "In Jerusalem I will put my Name." In both courts of the temple of the LORD, he built altars to all the starry hosts. He sacrifices his own son in fire, practiced sorcery and divination, and consulted with mediums and spiritists. He did much evil in the eyes of the LORD, provoking him to anger.

He took the carved Asherah pole he had made and put it in the temple, of which the LORD had said to David and to his son Solomon, "In this temple and in Jerusalem, which I have chosen out of all the tribes of Israel, I will put my Name forever. I will not again make the feet of the Israelites wander from the land I gave their forefathers, if only they will be careful to do everything I commanded them and will keep the whole Law that my servant Moses gave them." But the people did not listen. Manasseh led them astray, so that they did more evil than the nations the LORD had destroyed before the Israelites.

The LORD said through his servants the prophets: "Manasseh king of Judah has committed these detestable sins. He has done more evil than the Amorites who preceded him and has led Judah into sin with his idols. Therefore this is what the LORD, the God of Israel, says: I am going to bring such disaster on Jerusalem and Judah that the ears of everyone who hears of it will tingle. I will stretch out over Jerusalem the measuring line used against Samaria and the plumb line used against the house of Ahab. I will wipe out Jerusalem as one wipes a dish, wiping it and turning it upside down. I will forsake the remnant of my inheritance and hand them over to their enemies. They will be looted and plundered by all their foes, because they have done evil in my eyes and have provoked me to anger from the day their forefathers came out of Egypt until this day."

Moreover, Manasseh also shed so much innocent blood that he filled Jerusalem from end to end—besides the sin that he had caused Judah to commit, so that they did evil in the eyes of the LORD.

As for the other events of Manasseh's reign, and all he did, including the sin he committed, are they not written in the book of the annals of the kings of Judah? Manasseh rested with his fathers and was buried in his palace garden, the garden of Uzza. And Amon his son succeeded him as king.

Amon was twenty-two years old when he became king, and he reigned in Jerusalem two years. His mother's name was Meshullemeth daughter of Haruz; she was from Jotbah. He did evil in the eyes of the LORD, as his father Manasseh had done. He walked in all the ways of his father; he worshiped the idols his father had worshiped, and bowed down to them. He forsook the LORD, the God of his fathers, and did not walk in the way of the LORD.

Amon's officials conspired against him and assassinated the king in his palace. Then the people of the land killed all who had plotted against King Amon, and they made Josiah his son king in his place.

As for the other events of Amon's reign, and what he did, are they not written in the book of the annals of the kings of Judah? He was buried in his grave in the garden of Uzza. And Josiah his son succeeded him as king.

Josiah was eight years old when he became king, and he reigned in Jerusalem thirty-one years. His mother is Jedidah daughter of Adaiah; she was from Bozkath. He did what was right in the eyes of the LORD and walked in all the ways of his father David, not turning aside to the right or to the left.

In the eighteenth year of his reign, King Josiah sent the secretary, Shaphan son of Azaliah, the son of Meshullam, to the temple of the LORD. He said: "Go up to Hilkiah the high priest and have him get ready the money that has been brought into the temple of the LORD, which the doorkeepers have collected from the people. Have them entrust it to the men appointed to supervise the work on the temple. And have these men pay the workers who repair the temple of the LORD–the carpenters, the builders and the masons. Also have them purchase timber and dressed stone to repair the temple. But they need not account for the money entrusted to them, because they are acting faithfully.

Hilkiah the high priest said to Shaphan the secretary, "I have found the Book of the Law in the temple of the LORD." He gave it to Shaphan, who read it. Then Shaphan the secretary went to the king and reported to him: "Your officials have paid out the money that was in the temple of the LORD and have entrusted it to the workers and supervisors of the temple." Then Shaphan the secretary informed the king, "Hilkiah the priest has given me a book." And Shaphan read from it in the presence of the king.

When the king heard the words of the Book of the Law, he tore his robes. He gave these orders to Hilkiah the priest, Ahikam son of Shaphan, Acbor son of Micaiah, Shaphan the secretary and Asaiah the king's attendant: "Go and inquire of the LORD for me and for the people and for all Judah about what is written in this book that has been found. Great is the LORD's anger that burns against us because our fathers have not obeyed the words of this book; they have not acted in accordance with all that is written there concerning us."

Hilkiah the priest, Ahikam, Acbor, Shaphan and Asaiah went to speak to the prophetess Huldah, who was the wife of Shallum son of Tikvah, the son of Harhas, keeper of the wardrobe. She lived in Jerusalem, in the Second District.

She said to them, "This is what the LORD, the God of Israel says: Tell the man who sent you to me, "This is what the LORD says: I am going to bring disaster on this place and its people, according to everything written in the book the king of Judah read. Because they have forsaken me and burned incense to others gods and provoked me to anger by all the idols their hands have made, my anger will burn against this place and will not be quenched. Tell the king of Judah, who sent you to inquire of the LORD, This is what the Lord, the God of Israel, says concerning the words you have heard: Because your heart was responsive and you humbled yourself before the LORD when you heard what I have spoken against this place and its people, that they would become accursed and laid waste, and because you tore your robes and wept in my presence, I have heard you, declares the LORD. Therefore I will gather you to your fathers, and you will be buried in peace. Your eyes will not see all the disaster I am going to bring on this place." So they took her answer back to the king.

Then the king called together all the elders of Judah and Jerusalem. He went up to the temple of the LORD with the men of Judah, the people of Jerusalem, the priests and the prophets—all the people from the least to the greatest.

He read in their hearing all the words of the Book of the Covenant, which had been found in the temple of the LORD. The king stood by the pillar and renewed the covenant in the presence of the LORD–to follow the LORD and keep his commands, regulations and decrees with all his heart and all his soul, thus confirming the words of the covenant written in this book. Then all the people pledged themselves to the covenant.

2 Kings 21:1–23:4

"He did much evil in the eyes of the Lord," means that Manasseh sought out evil in every possible way. He placed it in office. He endeavored to become acquainted with all the heathen religions he could find and introduced them into Judah. We can see how sin perpetuates itself. There is a progressive nature to sin. God was angered because they demonstrate lack of faith, sin and open the doors to demonic attack. However, in the story we can see the power of penitent prayer. We see here that no one is too great a sinner to pray to God for mercy. It is rare to find a king in the Old Testament who obeyed God completely. Josiah was such a person, and he was only eight years old when he began to reign. We need to remember that children are the future leaders of our churches and our worlds. They may have to wait until they are adults to do the work God has laid out for them, but they are never too young to take God seriously and obey Him.

When God's word was found, Josiah began to make drastic changes to bring his kingdom into line with God's commands. Today we have God's Word at our fingertips. How much change must we make in order to bring our lives into line with God's Word? When Josiah realized the terrible state of Judah's religious life, he did something about it; it is not enough to say we believe what is right, we must respond with action, doing what faith requires. (*Life Application Bible*, pg. 650)

Manasseh was twelve years old when he became king and he reigned in Jerusalem fifty-five- years. He did evil in the eyes of the Lord, following the detestable practices of the nations the LORD had driven out before the Israelites. He rebuilt the high places his father Hezekiah had demolished; he also erected altars to the Baals and made Asherah poles. He bowed down to all the starry hosts and worshiped them. He built altars in the temple of the LORD, of which the LORD had said, "My Name will remain in Jerusalem forever." In both courts of the temple of the LORD, he built altars to all the starry hosts. He sacrificed his sons in the fire in the Valley of Ben Hinnom, practiced sorcery, divination and witchcraft, and consulted mediums and spiritists. He did much evil in the eyes of the LORD, provoking him to anger. He took the carved image he had made and put it in God's temple, of which God had said to David and to his son Solomon, "In this temple and in Jerusalem, which I have chosen out of all the tribes of Israel, I will put my Name forever. I will not again make the feet of the Israelites leave the land. I assigned to your forefathers, if only they will be careful to do everything I commanded them concerning all the laws, decrees and ordinances given through Moses." But Manasseh led Judah and the people of Jerusalem astray, so that they did more evil than the nations the LORD had destroyed before the Israelites. The LORD spoke to Manasseh and his people, but they paid no attention. So the LORD brought against them the army commanders of the king of Assyria, who took Manasseh prisoner, put a hook in his nose, bound him with bronze shackles and took him to Babylon. In his distress he sought the favor of the LORD his God and humbled himself greatly before the God of his fathers. And when he prayed to him, the LORD was moved by his entreaty and listened to his plea; so he brought him back to Jerusalem and to his kingdom. Then Manasseh knew that the LORD is God.

2 Chronicles 33:1–13

Manasseh participated in every form of evil. Part of the evil that he did was to undo the good that had been done before him as well as persuading and seducing the people to sin. But upon heartfelt repentance God showed mercy and forgave him. How far has God gone to get our attention? God's forgiveness comes when we repent and pray. God gives us a new attitude.

You have abandoned your people, the house of Jacob. They are full of superstitions from the East; they practice divination like the Philistines and clasp hands with pagans. **Isaiah 2:6**

The superstitions from the East consisted of practicing sorcery and divination, and consulting with mediums and spiritists. "Divination like the Philistines" means claiming to know and control the future (*Life Application Bible*, pg. 1172). This comes from the power of demons or by interpreting omens from evil spirits.

---

*When men tell you to consult mediums and spiritists,
who whisper and mutter, should not a people inquire of
their God? Why consult the dead on behalf of the living?*
Isaiah 8:19

This is a rebuke to those who are giving themselves over to
spiritism and a command to turn only to the Word of God for
guidance and light. The people consult mediums and spiritists
to seek answers instead of consulting God. God alone knows the
future. We can trust God to guide us (*Life Application Bible*, pg.
1183). God alone knows the future and only He is eternal. If we
have questions about life after death, the answer is not with mediums or those who say they can consult with the dead. The answer
is in the Word of God and through the blood of Jesus Christ.

---

*"Now then, listen, you wanton creature, lounging in your
security and saying to yourself, 'I am, and there is none
beside me. I will never be a widow or suffer the loss of
children.' Both of these will overtake you in a moment,
or a single day: loss of children and widowhood. They
will come upon you in full measure, in spite of your many
sorceries and all your potent spells. You have trusted in
your wickedness and have said, 'No one sees me.' Your
wisdom and knowledge mislead you when you say to
yourself, I am, and there is none beside me. Disaster will
come upon you, and you will not know how to conjure
it away. A calamity will fall upon you that you cannot
ward off with a ransom, a catastrophe you cannot foresee*

will suddenly come upon you. Keep on, then, with your magic spells and with your many sorceries, which you have labored at since childhood. Perhaps you will succeed, perhaps you will cause terror. All the counsel you have received has only worn you out. Let your astrologers come forward, those stargazers who make predictions month by month, let them save you from what is coming upon you. **Isaiah 47:8–13**

Many aspects of our society can lead us to be addicted to wealth, pleasures and power, but these all will pass away (*Life Application Bible*, pg. 1250). In the scripture they relied on everything but God. Only God can deliver us. How responsible for the gifts and talents God has given us are we? When and what do we rely upon?

. . . and say, "This is what the Sovereign LORD says: Woe to the women who sew magic charms on all their wrists and make veils of various lengths for their heads in order to ensnare people. Will you ensnare the lives of my people but preserve your own? You have profaned me among my people for a few handfuls of barley and scraps of break. By lying to my people, who listen to lies, you have killed those who should not have died and spared those who should not live. Therefore this is what the Sovereign LORD says: I am against your magic charms with which you ensnare people like birds and I will tear them from your arms; I will set free the people that you ensnare like birds. I will tear off your veils and save my people from your hands, and they will no longer fall prey

to your power. Then you will know that I am the LORD. Because you disheartened the righteous with your lies, when I had brought them no grief, and because you encouraged the wicked not to turn from their evil ways and so save their lives, therefore you will no longer see false visions or practice divination. I will save my people from your hands. And then you will know that I am the LORD. **Ezekiel 13:18–23**

Charms are used as a process of sympathetic magic in which the wearer believes they have extra strength or power but can be used by occultists to bind the wearer. Charms, which can look harmless, can be used by Satan to ensnare us.

Now for some time a man named Simon had practiced sorcery in the city and amazed all the people of Samaria. He boasted that he was someone great, and all the people, both high and low, gave him their attention and exclaimed, "this man is the divine power known as the Great Power." They followed him because he had amazed them for a long time with his magic. **Acts 8:9–11**

False Messiahs worked wonders, healings, exorcisms, these may have been magic tricks or they may have been empowered by Satan.

Many of those who believed now came and openly confessed their evil deeds. A number who had practiced sorcery brought their scrolls together and burned them publicly. When they calculated the value of the scrolls, the total came to fifty thousand drachmas. **Acts 19:18–19**

You cannot be a believer and hold on to the occult, black magic or sorcery. Once you begin to dabble, it is extremely easy to become obsessed because Satan is very powerful (*Life Application Bible*, pg. 2002). The Ephesians got rid of everything that could keep them trapped in the practice. What do we have in our life that is so important that we believe it to be worth a great deal or have values vested with emotional, physical or financial desires?

The acts of the sinful nature are obvious; sexual immorality, impurity and debauchery; idolatry and witchcraft; hatred, discord, jealousy, fits of rage, selfish ambition, dissensions, factions and envy; drunkenness, orgies, and the like. I warn you, as I did before, that those who live like this will not inherit the kingdom of God. **Galatians 5:19–21**

Scripture does not list all possible sins but lists them in four categories of sensual passions, dealing with things evil, violations of brotherly love and intemperate excesses. We all have evil desires and we cannot just ignore them. In following the Holy Spirit, we must deal with them decisively.

Rejecting Christ/Blaspheme Of The Holy Spirit

All of my life I have heard that suicide was an unforgivable sin. The more I study and research, the more I reject this belief. Suicide is defined as death at one's own hand. But nowhere in scripture is it listed as *the* unforgivable sin.

Those who believe suicide is the unforgivable sin, cite the scripture of Judas hanging himself. However, the scripture in this chapter show that the unforgivable sin is in rejecting Christ. Luke 22:3 states that Satan entered Judas. Judas himself opened the door that he could not afterward close. We need to remember that Satan is a legal expert. When some sinful act has opened the way for a demon, it will not leave until the sinful act has been confessed and canceled by God's forgiveness. It is not a single act that opens the door. (Prince, *They Shall Expel Demons, pg. 108)*

Virtually every suicide, I believe, is motivated by a demon. It is obvious that a demon of suicide does not enter because a person has already killed themselves. It comes to drive a person to suicide. This is true of a demon of murder. It does not come in because a person has already committed murder. Rather it enters to drive a person to commit murder. Remember, the Bible defines murder primarily as an inner attitude: 1 John 3:15 says; *"Whoever hates his brother is a murderer"* (Prince, *They Shall Expel Demons*, pg. 181).

Both Peter and Judas betrayed Christ. One was forgiven and the other was not. Why? Both felt remorse, but only Peter repented. It was in attitude that Peter was forgiven.

Mark 3:28 below shows that the only eternal sin is blaspheme against the Holy Spirit. Remember that demons are invisible. They cannot be perceived by human eyes. We can, however, recognize their presence and activity in the same way that we recognize the presence of the wind. Actually, this is an appropriate comparison because in both Hebrew and Greek, the word for spirit is also the word for wind. We never actually see the wind, but we see the effects the wind produces: dust rising in the streets, clouds sailing across the sky, trees all bending in one direction, rain being driven across our field of vision. All these signposts reveal the presence and activity of the wind.

So it is with demons. We do not normally see them, but we recognize their presence by certain characteristic actions. One such action is the whisper of the accusing demon which says; "you've committed the unforgivable sin." When a person is assailed by this thought, we must remember that this is nothing but an accusation of a lying spirit. If we had really committed the unforgivable sin, we would be so hardened that we wouldn't care. The fact that we are concerned with it proves that we have not committed it. (Prince, *They Shall Expel Demons*, pg. 168)

> *I tell you the truth, all the sins and blasphemies of men will be forgiven them. But whoever blasphemes against the Holy Spirit will never be forgiven; he is guilty of eternal sin. He said this because they were saying, "He has an evil spirit."*
> **Mark 3:28–30**

The unpardonable sin is not an isolated act or utterance, but an attitude of defiance and deliberate rejection of light, a preference of darkness to light. This is the unforgivable sin. As Christians, we need not worry about this. This sin is attributing to

Satan what is the work of the Holy Spirit. It is a heart attitude of unbelief and un-repentance. This is deliberate and ongoing rejection of the work of the Holy Spirit; it rejects God himself (*Life Application Bible*, pg. 1733).

. . . and to put on the new self, created to be like God in true righteousness and holiness. Therefore each of you must put off falsehood and speak truthfully to his neighbor, for we are all members of one body, In your anger do not sin. Do not let the sun go down while you are still angry, and do not give the devil a foothold. He who has been stealing must steal no longer, but must work, doing something useful with his own hands, that he may have something to share with those in need. Do not let any unwholesome talk come out of your mouths, but only what is helpful for building others up according to their needs, that it may benefit those who listen. And do not grieve the Holy Spirit of God, with whom you were sealed for the day of redemption. Get rid of all bitterness, rage and anger, brawling and slander, along with every form of malice. Be kind and compassionate to one another, forgiving each other, just as in Christ God forgave you.
Ephesians 4:24–32

God's children are told not to grieve the Spirit. This means we are not to hurt or offend Him by sin. When we sin, the Spirit convicts us, thereby drawing our attention to the fact that it is wrong. When we ignore or suppress this work of the Spirit, we grieve Him. (Lightner, *Angels, Satan, and Demons*, pg. 114)

Righteous anger easily passes into resentment when personal

feelings begin to control it. To harbor personal anger or to keep even righteous anger too long is to let the devil have his own way in our lives. The list of sins in the scripture above can disrupt a faith community and invite Satan through open doors. Spiritual warfare can divide us. Are we grieving or pleasing God with our attitudes and actions? The Holy Spirit is God's seal that we belong to God. His power works in us to transform us. Therefore we should know this list and ask for the power of the Holy Spirit against it.

But mark this: There will be terrible times in the last days. People will be lovers of themselves, lovers of money, boastful, proud, abusive, disobedient to their parents, ungrateful, unholy, without love, unforgiving, slanderous, without self control, brutal, not lovers of the good, treacherous, rash, conceited, lovers of pleasure rather than lovers of God–having a form of godliness but denying its power. Have nothing to do with them.
2 Timothy 3:1–5

The idea is denying the power of God. The word "denying" is the Greek word *arneomia*, which means "I know the power exists, and I know it's real, but I'm going to stop its operation. It refers to the deliberate refusal of God's power. (Renner, *Seducing Spirits and Doctrine of Demons*, pg. 37) Paul's descriptive list of behavior in the last days describes our society, even some Christians. We must check our lives against Paul's list. Don't give in to societies' pressures. The "form" or appearance of godliness includes going to church, knowing Christian doctrine, using Christian language, following the traditions. Such practices make a person look good, but if the inner attitude of belief, love and worship are lacking, the outer appearance is meaningless. Paul warns us not to be deceived by people who only appear to be Christians. (*Life Application Bible*, pg. 2202)

> *If we deliberately keep on sinning after we have received the knowledge of the truth, no sacrifice for sins is left, but only a fearful expectation of judgment and of raging fire that will consume the enemies of God. Anyone who rejected the law of Moses died without mercy on the testimony of two or three witnesses. How much more severely do you think a man deserves to be punished who has trampled the Son of God under foot, who has treated as an unholy thing the blood of the covenant that sanctified him, and who has insulted the Spirit of grace?*
> Hebrews 10:26–29

If we willfully, persistently, and by deliberate choice, deny there is any significance to the blood of Christ and no sacrifice for sin because the final sacrifice had been rejected, this is the unforgivable sin. The meaning here is that Jesus will vindicate the true by removing the false. This warning was given to Jewish Christians who were tempted to reject Christ for Judaism, but it applies to anyone who rejects Christ for another religion or cult where Christ is not the center. There is no other acceptable sacrifice for sin than the death of Christ on the cross.

Spiritual Warfare/Resisting/ Rebuking Satan

Terry C. Hulbert lists the following factors that he feels have contributed to the spiritual warfare emphasis today.

A decrease in the knowledge of and respect for the Bible. Many evangelicals know little of what the Bible teaches and do not take its standards seriously. George Barna's research, reported in his book, *What Americans Believe*, showed that almost half the evangelicals in the United States deny the existence of Satan, seeing him only as a symbol of all that is evil.

A diminishing of the importance of biblical values among believers as determinative for belief and behavior, thus leaving them vulnerable to Satan's temptations.

The increased immigration of people who bring with them a variety of non-biblical (satanic) religions.

A trend toward pluralism, the relativistic, nonjudgmental attitude that denies absolutes and accepts contra-biblical beliefs as valid.

The secularization and trivialization of the events of the birth, death, and resurrection of Christ, and a mythologizing of God and Satan. The former detracts from the deity of Christ and the supreme significance of his life and work; the latter makes man himself the ultimate reality and deceives him by implying that he can control his own destiny in this life and after death.

An increased acceptance of a humanistic perspective in psychology and counseling and in popular attitudes which ignore the reality of God and the fact of sin.

An increased fascination and involvement with the occult, horoscopes, and New Age concepts and practices.

An increase in the sense of spiritual vacuum and loss of control resulting from secularism and humanism, which leads many to turn to occult practices.

The influence of recent literature, some speculative, some deceptive, which constitutes both a cause and an effect. In some cases the result has been positive, raising the level of awareness of satanic activity. The media, especially some movies, television programs, and music videos have also contributed to this trend.

The denial of sin as man's basic problem. Sin is essentially submission to Satan and rebellion against God, as it was in the beginning with Adam and Eve. (Hulbert, *Spiritual Warfare*, pg. 2–3)

The first step toward being a true warrior in Christ is to renounce all past or present involvement with any activity or group which denies Jesus Christ or offers guidance through any source other than the absolute authority of the Bible. (Anderson, *Winning Spiritual Warfare*, pg. 19)

God needs two things. Sometimes it is a physical need such as in scripture Jesus had need of a donkey. The encyclopedia said that a donkey is a burden bearer that carries a weight many times greater than its size. Sometimes it carries the man; sometimes it carries the man's burden. And often it walks alongside the man. Christ says His yoke is easy so like the donkey he walks beside us carrying our burdens. (Alves, *Becoming A Prayer Warrior*, pg. 73)

He is also in need of a channel. What's a channel? It's a tube through which water flows, or it's a conduit through which electricity flows. God channels His power through our spirit, past our soul, and out our bodies. To be a channel we must have surrendered ourselves to Christ. If we're built on a firm foundation of the Word, we know what is right and good. God is crying out for a body of people who will be a channel for His power. All He needs is a yielded vessel. (Renner, *Seducing Spirits and Doctrine of Demons*, pg. 45)

> *"You shall not make for yourself an idol in the form of anything in heaven above or on the earth beneath or in the waters below. You shall not bow down to them or worship them; for I, the LORD your God, am a jealous God, punishing the children for the sin of the fathers to the third and fourth generation of those who love me and keep my commandments."* Exodus 20:4–6

Iniquities can be passed on from one generation to the next if you don't renounce the sins of your ancestors and claim your new spiritual heritage in Christ. You are not guilty for the sin of any ancestor, but because of their sin, you may be vulnerable to Satan's attack.

Because of the fall, you are genetically predisposed to certain strengths or weaknesses and are influenced by the physical and spiritual atmosphere in which you were raised. These conditions can contribute toward causing someone to struggle with a particular sin.

> *For if you remain silent at this time, relief and deliverance for the Jews will arise from another place, but you and your father's family will perish. And who knows but that you have come to royal position for such a time as this?* Esther 4:14

When it is within our reach to save others, we must do so. In a life-threatening situation, don't withdraw, behave selfishly, wallow in despair, or wait for God to fix everything. Instead ask God for His direction and act. (*Life Application Bible*, pg. 829)

We never know why we might be at a place or for what purpose. Our actions can create ripples that can save those around us.

Who is a God like you, who pardons sin and forgives the transgression of the remnant of his inheritance? You do not stay angry forever but delight to show mercy. You will again have compassion on us; you will tread our sins underfoot and hurl all our iniquities into the depths of the sea. **Micah 7:18–19**

There are those who have endeavored to explain away the solemn fact of sin; who contend that there is no intentional preference of wrong to right. There is no escape from admitting the fact of sin. The Word declares that "all have sinned, and come short of the glory of God" (Romans 3:23).

Divine forgiveness includes deliverance from the consequences of sin. Every spiritual defeat works to weaken our moral strength. The power of human language is too weak to adequately describe the love of God as expressed even in the smallest detail. God seeks us out to show us mercy. This is a continual action on the part of God. Isolated acts of pardon are not the case with God. It is a joy to God to forgive and save.

One of the marked peculiarities of Divine forgiveness is the result on the sinner themselves. Think about those you have forgiven. There are times when we are disappointed in those we have forgiven. Not so with God. Whenever he forgives sins he reforms the sinner.

Then God casts the sins, not into the shallow parts of the sea, where they will be subject to the tidal waves which might bring them back into sight, but into the depths of the seas. Such is Gods matchless mercy.

The question then becomes: How can God be just and yet our justifier? This mystery, which lies at the root of His character, finds its only answer in the cross of Christ. God's laws are eternal and inexorable. He cannot swerve from absolute righteousness. Sin must bring shame, misery and death now and in the hereafter.

If, therefore, God had said all shall be overlooked, the penalty shall be removed, the Law repealed, it would appear to intelligent people, that the Law was either unjust from the beginning or unjust in its repeal. It is in the perfect integrity and mercy of God that gives us the foundation of hope. The Son of God became the Son of Man. He gathered to Himself all our sin, vindicating the Law by His obedience, and dying on the cross for our transgressions.

God delights to show mercy. He does not forgive grudgingly, but is glad when we repent and offers forgiveness to all who come back to him. Today we can confess our sins and receive His loving forgiveness. We should not be too proud to accept God's free offer. (*Life Application Bible*, pg. 1578)

As soon as Jesus was baptized, he went up out of the water. At that moment heaven was opened, and he saw the Spirit of God descending like a dove and lighting on him. And a voice from heaven said, "This is my Son, whom I love; with him I am well pleased.
Matthew 3:16–17

All three persons of the Trinity are present, either visible or audible to human eyes or ears at this sacred moment. Jesus

147

as human, the Holy Spirit in the form of a dove, and God the Father through His voice. Jesus, in this scripture, is fully human but notice the words of God, "This is my Son, whom I love; with him I am well pleased." This does not mean that Jesus was not one with the Spirit from birth. Jesus is fully divine as well. Jesus chose to be baptized by water. Immediately following being baptized with water, God baptized Him with the Holy Spirit. The Spirit came to equip Him for His public ministry. It is through the indwelling of the Holy Spirit of God that Jesus, the man, was able to resist and rebuke Satan. If Jesus needed to be baptized with water and the Holy Spirit in order to live and to resist Satan, don't we? (Rogerson, *The Angels of God*, handout) The very Spirit, who enabled and empowered Jesus, God has given to us. We need to imitate the Lord Jesus, use all the means of grace offered. Pray for fuller gifts of the Holy Spirit.

Then Jesus was led by the Spirit into the desert to be tempted by the devil. After fasting forty days and forty nights, he was hungry. The tempter came to him and said, "If you are the Son of God, tell these stones to become bread." Jesus answered, "It is written: 'Man does not live on bread alone, but on every word that comes from the mouth of God.'" Then the devil took him to the holy city and had him stand on the highest point of the temple. "If you are the Son of God," he said, "throw yourself down. For it is written: "He will command his angels concerning you, and they will lift you up in their hands, so that you will not strike your foot against a stone.'" Jesus answered him, "It is also written: 'Do not put the Lord your God to the test.'" Again, the devil took him to

a very high mountain and showed him all the kingdoms
of the world and their splendor. "All this I will give you,"
he said, "if you will bow down and worship me." Jesus
said to him, "Away from me, Satan! For it is written:
'Worship the Lord your God, and serve him only.'" Then
the devil left him, and angels came and attended him.
Matthew 4:1–11

In verse 5 the Greek word, *logos*, in its various forms, is rendered, "holu," "holiness," "sanctify," and "sanctified." Like the Hebrew word *qodesh*, it signifies something or someone set apart. In verse 8 the Greek word *kosmos*, means order. Sometimes *kosmos* means earth. When *kosmos* is used in the New Testament for humanity, the world of men, it denotes organized humanity, humanity in families, tribes, and nations. The word for chaotic unorganized humanity, the mere mass of men, is *thalassa*, the sea of men. The word for world, *kosmos*, is used in the bad ethical sense. (*New Scofield Study Bible*, pg. 1322)

It is commonly said that the Savior was confronted with three different temptations from Satan in the wilderness experience. I believe it is better to view the three solicitations of Satan as three different attempts to get the Savior to commit the one sin of acting independently of God the Father's will for Him. After all, Satan himself had sinned by acting independently of God as seen in his "I wills." Throughout Old Testament history the story is repeated over and over. In sinning, people are rebelling against God and His will. (Lightner, *Angels, Satan, and Demons*, pg. 107)

The Word of God is a powerful weapon, and we must never let it slip or become dull. Jesus thrust Satan with the Sword of the Spirit with Scripture. The devil will try in every way that he can to convince the Christian warrior to substitute something else in place of the Word. Psychology and worldly counsel will not phase the devil. Stand on the Word of God. Joshua was instructed by God on how to guarantee success in warfare: "do not let the Word of God depart out of your mouth, meditate upon it day and night and do what God's Word says" (Joshua 1:8).

Remember, Satan uses Scripture against those who stand on the Word. He can tempt those who respect the Word to follow the letter of the law rather than the Spirit of the law, for he knows very well that the letter of the law kills and the spirit of the law gives life. (Hammond, *Demons and Deliverance*, pg. 7)

There is a close connection between the baptism and the temptation. By the former, Jesus dedicated Himself to the way of the cross. In the latter, the devil presented to His mind ways of carrying out His ministry, which would have avoided the cross. The Holy Spirit led Jesus into the desert. This was a preparatory time for the ministry that was to come. The express purpose of the desert trip was so Jesus could be tempted by the devil. His entire ministry depended on the outcome of His encounter with the devil.

The tests were a demonstration of the impossibility of Jesus failing. The tempter only came to Jesus when Jesus had fasted for forty days and nights, when he was at his weakest. This was a demonstration that at Jesus weakest, the Lord could meet and conquer the devil at his strongest.

A person cannot show true obedience if they have not been tempted, and have an opportunity to disobey. Again, temptation is not a sin. Temptation comes when we are most vulnerable, tired, hungry, alone, under physical or emotional stress and through our strengths, where pride is. When tempted, look at whether Satan is trying to block God's purpose for you, or for someone else's life. The devil said the entire world belonged to him. Jesus didn't argue with him but refused to validate his belief. Jesus knows the world will be redeemed through His blood that was shed on the cross. The devil offers us the world by trying to entice us with material things and power. The devil is persevering; and only persevering in that resistance can overcome him. If he does not succeed in one way, he will try another. In dark moments, we cannot trust our own thoughts, temptations can be sophisticated. We can resist temptation the same way Jesus did by quoting scripture. "Depart from me Satan; Worship the Lord your God and serve Him only.

After Satan departed, angels came and ministered to him. At that point Jesus was free from Satan's incessant wiles and snares and won freedom from him. We may also win some respite from Satan, if we faithfully follow our Lord in resisting temptation.

Jesus went throughout Galilee, teaching in their synagogues, preaching the good news of the kingdom, and healing every disease and sickness among the people. News about him spread all over Syria, and people brought to him all who were ill with various diseases, those suffering sever pain, the demon possessed, those having seizures, and the paralyzed, and he healed them. Large crowds from Galilee, the Decapolis, Jerusalem, Judea and the region across the Jordan followed him.
Matthew 4:23–25

Christ can heal us, not just of physical sickness, but of spiritual sickness as well. There's no sin or problem too great or too small for him to handle. (*Life Application Bible*, pg. 1651)

Through Jesus the Gospel of the Kingdom was proclaimed and manifest. His Gospel includes healing and deliverance. Those who were demonized were healed through deliverance. The Greek word for healed in verse twenty-four is *therapeuo*, which literally means the care and attendance necessary to bring one back to wholeness. Therapeuo strongly suggests a process of deliverance.

"When you fast, do not look somber as the hypocrites do, for they disfigure their faces to show men they are fasting. I tell you the truth, they have received their reward in full." **Matthew 6:16**

Jesus wants us to adopt spiritual disciplines for the right reasons, not from selfish desires for praise. (*Life Application Bible*, pg. 1658)

Fasting is a spiritual discipline which every Christian is expected to practice. Jesus did not say "if you fast; He said when you fast." (Hammond, *Demons and Deliverance*, pg. 6)

Most people make the assumption that they must fast for long periods of time. A fast can be only through one meal of which the time is spent in focused mediation or study of Christ, the Scriptures and His will for us.

When evening came, many who were demon-possessed were brought to him, and he drove out the spirits with a word and healed all the sick. **Matthew 8:16**

Jesus has authority over all evil powers and all earthly diseases. (*Life Application Bible*, pg. 1663)

It is a widespread error of belief that Jesus never commanded an evil spirit more than once. However, there is no article in the

Greek text. The text literally says: "He cast out the spirits with Word." In contrast to the Jewish exorcists, who used incantations, herbs and occult paraphernalia, Jesus spoke authoritatively to demons and they obey Him. In the case of the Gadarene, Jesus commanded the demon repeatedly.

Demons are personalities. Like people, some unclean spirits are stronger willed than others, and therefore, slower to respond to orders given. Too, our warfare against demon spirits is a wrestling conflict whereby continuous pressure is placed upon them until they are defeated. Repeat commands given to demons, keep spiritual pressure upon them until they yield.

We are not to suppose that commanding a demon more than once is a negative reflection upon our faith but rather a witness to the quality of our faith. True faith is persistent and active, not presumptuous and passive. (Hammond, *Demons and Deliverance*, pg. 35)

"Or again, how can anyone enter a strong man's house and carry off his possessions unless he first ties up the strong man? Then he can rob his house." **Matthew 12:29**

At Jesus' birth, Satan's power and control were disrupted. Jesus has complete power and authority over Satan and all his forces. (*Life Application Bible*, pg. 1674)

One never faces a demon except in the sense of a strong man. Each demon has direct connections with the demonic kingdom. Demons want nothing to do with Jesus. They have nothing in common with Him. They do not want an open confrontation with either Jesus or with His disciples who bear His authority. (Hammond, *Demons and Deliverance*, pg. 19)

When Jesus came to the region of Caesarea Philippi, he asked his disciples, "Who do people say the Son of Man is?" They replied, "Some say John the Baptist; others say Elijah; and still others, Jeremiah or one of the prophets." "But what about you?" he asked. "Who do you say I am?" Simon Peter answered, "You are the Christ, the Son of the living God." Jesus replied, "Blessed are you, Simon son of Jonah, for this was not revealed to you by man, but by my Father in heaven. And I tell you that you are Peter, and on this rock I will build my church, and the gates of Hades will not overcome it. I will give you the keys of the kingdom of heaven; whatever you bind on earth will be bound in heaven, and whatever you loose on earth will be loosed in heaven. **Matthew 16:13–19**

The religious leaders thought they held the keys of the kingdom, and they used them to shut some people out. To all who believe in Christ and obey His words, the kingdom doors are swung wide open. (*Life Application Bible*, pg. 1685)

Jesus raised the question as to His true identity. Jesus asked the question for a reason. What He was about to teach them required that they first know unequivocally who He is. His name is synonymous with His authority. We must know this truth in order to understand His church and its mission of spiritual warfare.

Jesus has provided His church with the keys of the Kingdom of Heaven by which His church will accomplish its victory. These keys are the power to bind and loose. Keys are the symbols of authority. For example, if you have the keys to an automobile, you can loose it by unlocking the door, starting the engine and driving away. Or you can use your keys to bind the automobile by shutting off the engine and locking the doors. The church is given authority to control the activities of the evil principalities and powers in the heavens.

These keys do not, as sometimes interpreted, represent authority to enter the Kingdom of Heaven, but rather the ability to function in Kingdom authority. They are keys "of" the Kingdom, rather than keys "to" the Kingdom. (Hammond, *Demons and Deliverance*, pg 104)

"If your brother sins against you, go and show him his fault, just between the two of you. If he listens to you, you have won your brother over. But if he will not listen, take one or two others along, so that every matter may be established by the testimony of two or three witnesses. If he refuses to listen to them, tell it to the church; and if he refuses to listen even to the church, treat him as you would a pagan or a tax collector. I tell you the truth, whatever you bind on earth will be bound in heaven, and whatever you loose on earth will be loosed in heaven."
Matthew 18:15–18

There are only two times in the New Testament where Jesus used the word "church." In both contexts Jesus immediately follows His reference to His church by a declaration of His church's power to bind and loose. It is an awesome responsibility of church authority to loose Satan to deal with those who refuse to submit to church discipline. (Hammond, *Demons and Deliverance*, pg. 118)

These are Jesus' guidelines for dealing with those who sin against us. They were meant for Christians, not unbelievers, sins committed against you, not others, and conflict resolution in the context of the church, not the community at large. Jesus' words are not a license for a frontal attack on every person who hurts or slights us.

When someone wrongs us, we often do the opposite of what Jesus recommends. We turn away in hatred or resentment, seek revenge, or engage in gossip. This opens the door to Satan in our community of faith. By contrast, we should go to that person first, as difficult as that may be. Then we should forgive that person as often as needed. The binding and loosing refers to the decisions of the church in conflicts. (*Life Application Bible*, pg. 1689)

Jesus replied, "Love the Lord your God with all your heart and with all your soul and with all your mind." This is the first and greatest commandment. **Matthew 22:37**

Who or what is most important to us becomes that which we worship. Our thoughts, love, devotion, trust, adoration, and obedience are directed to this object above all others. This object of worship is truly our God or god(s).

We were created to worship the true and living God. In fact, the Father seeks those who will worship Him in spirit and in truth (John 4:23). As children of God, "we know also that the Son of God has come and has given us understanding, so that we may know him who is true. And we are in him who is true, even in his Son Jesus Christ. He is the true God and eternal life" (I John 5:20).

The apostle John follows the above passage with a warning: "Little children, guard yourselves from idols (I John 5:21). An idol is a false god; any object of worship other than the true God.

Though we may not bow down to statues, it is easy for people and things of this world to subtly become more important to us than the Lord. The following prayer expresses the commitment of a heart that chooses to "worship the Lord God, and serve Him only" (Matthew 4:10).

Showing love means absolute devotion to the interests of another. This scripture goes directly to our state of mind. This is the most important place to start. It keeps us focused on Christ and on his love.

> *"Dear Lord God, I know how easy it is to allow other things and other people to become more important to me than You. I also know that this is terribly offensive to Your holy eyes, as You have commanded that I "shall have no other gods" before You.*
>
> *I confess to You that I have not loved you with all my heart and soul and mind. As a result, I have sinned against You, violating the first and greatest commandment. I repent of and turn away from this idolatry and now choose to return to You, Lord Jesus, as my first love.*
>
> *Please reveal to my mind now any and all idols in my life. I want to renounce each of them, and in so doing, cancel out any and all ground Satan may have gained in my life through my idolatry. In the name of Jesus, the true God. Amen." (Anderson. The Steps to Freedom in Christ, pg. 25)*

> *Then Jesus came to them and said, "All authority in heaven and on earth has been given to me. Therefore go and make disciples of all nations, baptizing them in the*

> name of the Father and of the Son and of the Holy Spirit,
> and teaching them to obey everything I have commanded
> you. And surely I am with you always, to the every end of
> the age. **Matthew 28:18–20**

In the progress of revelation the one true God appears clearly in the New Testament as existing in the three divine persons: named here "the Father," and "the Son," and "the Holy Spirit." Each of these divine persons possesses His own personal characteristics and is clearly distinguished from the others. Yet three persons are equal in being, power, and glory: Each being called "God"; each possessing all the divine attributes; each performing divine works and each receiving divine honors. A general formula as to how they function is as follows: from the Father, through the Son, by the Holy Spirit and to the Father. Even so, however, no one of the persons of the Trinity acts independently of the other persons; there is always mutual concurrence. (*New Scofield Bible*, pg. 1381)

Jesus' words affirm the reality of the Trinity. Some people accuse theologians of making up the concept of the Trinity and reading it into the Scriptures. As we see in this text, the concept comes directly from Jesus himself. He did not say baptize them into the names, but into the name of the Father, the Son and the Holy Spirit.

The disciples were to baptize people because baptism unites a believer with Jesus Christ, in his or her death to sin and resurrection, to new life. Baptism symbolizes submission to Christ, and a willingness to live God's way, and identification with God's covenant people.

How is Jesus with us? Jesus continues to be with us through the Holy Spirit. (*Life Application Bible*, pg. 1721)

The last words of someone dying are taken very seriously and at times literally by the law. These were Jesus' last words, how important they are, and how important it is to listen and act upon those words. How slow and reluctant have we been to carry out this commission? The existence of millions in the world today who have never heard the Savior's name is a disgrace to us all.

They went to Capernaum, and when the Sabbath came, Jesus went into the synagogue and began to teach. The people were amazed at his teaching, because he taught him as one who had authority, not as the teachers of the law. Just then a man in their synagogue who was possessed by an evil spirit cried out, "What do you want with us, Jesus of Nazareth? Have you come to destroy us? I know who you are, the Holy One of God!" "Be quiet!" said Jesus sternly. "Come out of him!" The evil spirit shook the man violently and came out of him with a shriek. The people were all so amazed that they asked each other, "What is this? A new teaching, and with authority. He even gives orders to evil spirits and they obey him." News about him spread quickly over the whole region of Galilee.
Mark 1:21–28

Teaching is a necessary balance to the ministry of deliverance, and is often the prelude to deliverance. Sound Bible teaching exposes the enemy. The specific scripture that Jesus was teaching was not stated, but we do know the subject excited the demons in the man demonized. (Hammond, *Demons and Deliverance*, pg. 14)

Evil spirits, or demons, are ruled by Satan. They work to tempt people to sin. Though not all disease comes from Satan, demons can cause a person to become mute, deaf, blind, or insane. But in every case where demons confront Jesus or were confronted by Jesus, they lost their power. (*Life Application Bible*, pg. 1727)

> . . . *and Jesus healed many who had various diseases. He also drove out many demons, but he would not let the demons speak because they knew who he was.*
>
> **Mark 1:34**

Jesus rebuked the spirit for speaking. Demons can be permitted to speak or be kept from speaking by those who have authority over them. Jesus stopped the spirit from speaking, for there was nothing to be gained by their words. Demons are anti-Christ in all that they say and do. Therefore, what they say is never a valid witness to the Person of Christ. We should never accept their testimony as a basis for validating any truth about Christ. (Hammond, *Demons and Deliverance*, pg. 20)

> *When they heard all he was doing, many people came to him from Judea, Jerusalem, Idumea, and the regions across the Jordan and around Tyre and Sidon. Because of the crowd he told His disciples to have a small boat ready for him to keep the people from crowding him. For he had healed many, so that those with diseases were pushing forward to touch him. Whenever the evil spirits saw him, they fell down before him and cried out, "You are the Son of God." But he gave them strict orders not to tell who he was. Jesus went up on a mountainside and called to him*

those he wanted, and they came to him. He appointed twelve, designating them apostles, that they might be with him and that he might send them out to preach and to have authority to drive out demons. **Mark 3:8–15**

Unclean spirits readily recognize Jesus as the Son of God while the Jewish nation as a whole could not decide upon His true identity. The demons had one advantage which men did not posses, for they knew that He was sinless, all their efforts to cause Him to sin had failed. Unclean spirits are forced to bow before Jesus. Here they "fell down before Him." Their acknowledgment was more than recognition: it was surrender.

Unclean spirits can be kept from speaking. Jesus charged them not to make Him known. Even when spirits speak truth, their testimony is not to be received. As important as it is for men to know who Jesus is, in order to believe in Him, the testimony of demons is not valid. Jesus consistently refused to accept any witness of Himself that came from demons.

Just as evil spirits recoil from Jesus' authority over them; they also tremble when confronted by Christian warriors who walk in discernment and faith. Wisdom dictates that we totally reject what evil spirits have to say. To do otherwise puts one in peril of the devil's snare of pride and deception. (Hammond, *Demons and Deliverance*, pg. 38)

The evil spirits knew Jesus was the Son of God, but they refused to turn from their evil purposes. Knowing about Jesus or even believing that He is God's Son, does not guarantee salvation. You must also want to follow and obey Him. Jesus wanted to teach the people about the kind of Messiah He really was, one who was far different from their expectations. Christ's Kingdom is spiritual. It begins not with the overthrow of governments, but with the overthrow of sin in people's hearts.

The disciples represented a wide range of backgrounds and life experiences, but apparently they had no more leadership potential than those who were not chosen. The one characteristic they all shared was their willingness to obey Jesus. We should not disqualify ourselves from service to Christ because we do not have the talents we believe we might need to succeed at the task. Being a good disciple is simply a matter of following Jesus with a willing heart. (*Life Application Bible*, pg. 8130)

Calling the twelve to him, he sent them out two by two and gave them authority over evil spirits. **Mark 6:7**

We can learn from the example of the disciples, Christ's power extends beyond His presence and can be delegated to us in His absence; and God can supply our temporal needs. The disciples were sent out in pairs. Individually we could cover more territory; however, as a team we can protect, strengthen, encourage and cover each other in prayer.

A man in the crowd answered, "Teacher, I brought you my son, who is possessed by a spirit that has robbed him of speech. Whenever it seizes him, it throws him to the ground. He foams at the mouth, gnashes his teeth and becomes rigid. I asked your disciples to drive out the spirit, but they could not." **Mark 9:17–18**

After Jesus had gone indoors, his disciples asked him privately, "Why couldn't we drive it out?" He replied, "This kind can come out only by prayer." **Mark 9:28–29**

One thing that strikes us is the controlled way that the father spoke to Jesus. He does not seem hostile about the fact that the disciples were unable to cure his son. He isn't bitter, just disappointed and discouraged, but still holding onto hope. Whatever the source of evil, human power is often unable to solve our problems. God himself doesn't always make our problems go away, but ultimately only God can help us deal with them. There are times when we will fail in our ministry. If we keep an open mind, we can learn from these failures. We say we are unlike the father in this text, we claim that we believe that Jesus can do anything, however our actions say we are like the father and we say to Jesus, "if you can . . ." (*Standard Lesson Commentary*, pg. 325).

The disciples had been given the necessary power so that they ought not to have failed, yet they found themselves helpless before the challenge of this need. It is easy to criticize the failure of others and do nothing ourselves. Why couldn't the disciples drive out this demon? Prayer is the key that unlocks faith in our lives. Effective prayer is both an attitude of complete dependence on God and the action of asking (*Life Application Bible*, pg. 1752). There is no need or sin beyond the power of Christ. By spiritual discipline, Christ's people may train themselves for grappling with every form of human misery and helplessness.

"And these signs will accompany those who believe: In my name they will drive out demons; they will speak in new tongues;" Mark 16:17

Just as surely as the Holy Spirit led Jesus into direct confrontation, the believer will also be led to face the devil, for the believer is commissioned to do so. Undoubtedly, few Christians have considered that it is God's plan that they also be in direct confrontation with the devil. Like Jesus we can win the battle. (Hammond, *Demons and Deliverance*, pg. 4)

He went down with them and stood on a level place. A large crowd of his disciples was there and a great number of people from all over Judea, from Jerusalem, and from the coast of Tyre and Sidon, who had come to hear him and to be healed of their diseases. Those troubled by evil spirits were cured, and the people all tried to touch him, because power was coming from him and healing them all. Luke 6:17–19

The ones delivered of unclean spirits are said to have been vexed, in the Greek, *ochleo*, troubled. *Soteria*, means deliverance. The full gospel of salvation includes not only the good news of deliverance from the penalty of sin but also the good news of deliverance from the power of unclean spirits and diseases. (Hammond, *Demons and Deliverance*, pg. 42)

Once word of Jesus' healing power spread, crowds gathered just to touch him. For many, he had become a symbol of good fortune, a lucky charm, or a magician. Instead of desiring God's pardon and love, they only wanted physical healing or a chance to see spectacular events. Some people still see God as a cosmic magician and consider prayer as a way to get God to do his tricks. But God is not a magician, he is the Master. Prayer is not a way for us to control God; it is a way for us to put ourselves under his control. (*Life Application Bible*, pg. 1806)

He replied, "I saw Satan fall like lightning from heaven. I have given you authority to trample on snakes and scorpions and to overcome all the power of the enemy; nothing will harm you. **Luke 10:18**

The disciples were enthusiastic over victories, but Jesus reminded them of the greatest victory, their names written in heaven. He warned them against pride which brought down the angel of darkness–Satan.

Then should not this woman, a daughter of Abraham, whom Satan has kept bound for eighteen long years, be set free on the Sabbath day from what bound her?
Luke 13:16

This text shows three things. The first is that Jesus called the woman to Him. This was unusual; generally, those whom He cured came to Him. He delivered her body from the spirit of infirmity that bound it. Jesus regarded God's great foe as the cause of human sickness and bodily impurity. The Pharisees hid behind law to avoid the obligations of love. In our world, there are many different diseases and illnesses. The good news is that Jesus is more powerful than any devil or any diseases. Satan is the origin of all illnesses, but Jesus still has the power to heal (*Life Application Bible*, pg. 1833). The second is that the walls of the synagogue did not protect her from demonic influences. Last is the fact that Christians can be afflicted by demons.

———————

> *To the Jews who had believed him, Jesus said, "IF you hold to my teaching, you are really my disciples. They you will know the truth, and the truth will set you free."*
> **John 8:31–32**

We are in no way dependent upon Satan's lies and half truths. Any help an evil spirit might give us can be obtained through the Holy Spirit. Which of these two sources of gaining knowledge glorifies God? (Hammond, *Demons and Deliverance*, pg. 21)

Jesus himself is the truth that sets us free. He is the source of truth, the perfect standard of what is right. He frees us from the consequences of sin, from self-deception, and from deception by Satan. He shows us clearly the way to eternal life with God. Thus Jesus does not give us freedom to do what we want, but freedom to follow God. As we seek to serve God, Jesus' perfect truth frees us to be all that God meant for us to be. (*Life Application Bible*, pg. 1894)

———————

> *My sheep listen to my voice; I know them, and they follow me. I give them eternal life, and they shall never perish; no one can snatch them out of my hand.*
> **John 10:27–28**

Satan does not have the power to harm our souls or take us away from God. Satan can try to lure us away but if we look to the power and authority of Jesus, he will protect us. We however, must learn to listen and hear the voice of God within us. If we do not listen and learn God's voice, how can we tell the difference between God's voice and that of Satan? Satan does not want us to hear God's voice because our partnership with the Lord can wreak havoc on his kingdom. Knowing that you will have to fight the enemy as you enter into your time of prayer alone with God will help you stay true to your commitment. (Alves, *Becoming A Prayer Warrior*, pg. 74)

And I will ask the Father, and he will give you another Counselor to be with you forever, the Spirit of truth. The world cannot accept him, because it neither sees him nor knows him. But you know him, for he lives with you and will be in you. **John 14:16**

In John 1:21 this word is translated "advocate." Christ is the Christian's advocate with the Father when the Christian sins; the Holy Spirit is our indwelling helper to help our ignorance and infirmity, and to make intercession for us. (*New Scofield Bible*, pg. 1506)

The function of the Spirit is to convince; to bear witness and to teach. This verse confirms the personality of the Spirit. The Spirit of truth will remain with us. When we are disturbed; we have a legacy and gift of His peace as a peace, which the world cannot give, or take away. The Holy Spirit is the very presence of God within us. This Spirit is stronger than Satan.

Some Jews who went around driving out evil spirits tried to invoke the name of the Lord Jesus over those who were demon-possessed. They would say, "In the name of Jesus, whom Paul preaches, I command you to come out." Seven sons of Sceva, a Jewish chief priest, were doing this. One day, the evil spirit answered them, "Jesus I know, and I know about Paul, but who are you?" Then the man who had the evil spirit jumped on them and overpowered them all. He gave them such a beating that they ran out of the house naked and bleeding. **Acts 19:13–16**

Demons know who Jesus is. At that point in time the demon in the man in Capernaum knew the identity of Jesus as the "Holy One of God." However, very few men of the time even suspected who He was. Likewise, demons also know and recognize the anointed servants of the Lord. (Hammond, *Demons and Deliverance*, pg. 20)

The power of the Holy Spirit is greater than the power of spells, charms and magic. Nothing can duplicate God's power. The power to change our lives comes from Christ.

In the same way, the Spirit helps us in our weakness. We do not know what we ought to pray for, but the Spirit himself intercedes for us with groans that words cannot express. **Romans 8:26**

As believers, we are not left to our own resources to cope with problems. Even when we don't know the right words to pray, the Holy Spirit prays with and for us, and God answers. With God helping us pray, we don't need to be afraid to come before Him. Ask the Holy Spirit to intercede "in accordance with God's will." Then, when we bring our requests before God, we can trust that he will always do what is best. (*Life Application Bible*, pg. 2042)

If you are like me you don't know what to pray the majority of the time. Let your prayers be spirit led. The word "helps" here describes how the Holy Spirit comes and picks us up and carries us to the throne of grace. If Satan can keep us in the dark, he can stunt our growth and make us ineffectual in our witness and ministry. We need to pray for each other continually that our vision will be clear to see and hear God's truth.

When you pray, Satan will try to interfere. So before you start to pray, bind his voice. Do this in the name of Jesus. Then trust the Holy Spirit. He will lead you and guide you into ALL truth. Our own will, at times, will get in the way of what the Spirit of the Lord wants to share with you or communicate with you. Lean on the understanding of the Holy Spirit.

After you have petitioned the Lord, take time to be still and wait upon Him. Don't be afraid of silence. Sometimes the Lord is silent. Don't become upset if you don't hear anything when you pray. Often the Holy Spirit just wants to worship the Lord. When you have your heart clean before Him, then there is nothing wrong. He just desires that you come and bask in His presence because you love Him and want to be with Him. Be still and know that He is God. (Alves, *Becoming a Prayer Warrior*, pg. 76)

Everyone must submit himself to the governing authorities, for there is no authority except that which God has established. The authorities that exist have been established by God. Consequently, he who rebels against the authority is rebelling against what God has instituted, and those who do so will bring judgment on themselves. For rulers hold no terror for those who do right, but for those who do wrong. Do you want to be free from fear of

> the one in authority? Then do what is right and he will commend you. For he is God's servant to do you good. But if you do wrong, be afraid, for he does not bear the sword for nothing. He is God's servant, an agent of wrath to bring punishment on the wrongdoer. Therefore, it is necessary to submit to the authorities, not only because of possible punishment but also because of conscience. This is also why you pay taxes, for the authorities are God's servants, who give their full time to governing. Give everyone what you owe him; if you owe taxes, pay taxes; if revenue, then revenue; if respect, then respect; if honor, then honor. **Romans 13:1–7**

We live in a rebellious age. Many people only obey laws and authorities when it is convenient for them. There is a general lack of respect for those in government, and Christians are often as guilty as the rest of society in fostering a critical, rebellious spirit. Certainly, we are not expected to agree with our leaders' policies that are in violation of Scripture, but we are to "honor all men; love the brotherhood, fear God, honor the king" (1 Peter 2:17). It is easy to believe the lie that those in authority over us are only robbing us of the freedom to do what we want. The truth is that God has placed them there for our protection and liberty. Rebelling against God and the authorities He has set up is a very serious sin for it gives Satan a wide open avenue to attack. Submission is the only solution. God requires more, however, than just the outward appearance of submission; He wants us to sincerely submit from the heart to those in authority. When you stand under the authority of God and those He has placed over you, you cut off this dangerous opening for demonic attacks.

The Bible makes it clear that we have two main responsibilities toward those in authority over us: to pray for them and to submit to them. To commit yourself to the godly lifestyle, pray the following prayer out loud from your heart:

> *Dear heavenly Father, You have said in the Bible that rebellion is the same thing as witchcraft and as bad as idolatry. I know I have not obeyed You in this area and have rebelled in my heart against You and against those You have placed in authority over me. Thank You for Your forgiveness of my rebellion. By the shed blood of the Lord Jesus Christ, I pray that all ground gained by evil spirits in my life due to my rebellion would be cancelled. I pray that You would show me all the ways I have been rebellious. I choose now to adopt a submissive spirit and a servant's heart. In Jesus' precious name, I pray. Amen (Anderson, The Bondage Breaker, pg. 199)*

Being under authority is clearly an act of faith! By submitting, you are trusting God to work through His established lines of authority, even when they are harsh or unkind or tell you to do something you don't want to do. There may be times when those over you abuse their authority and break the laws that are ordained by God for the protection of innocent people. In those cases, you will need to seek help from a *higher authority* for your protection. The laws in your state may require that such abuse be reported to the police or another governmental agency. If there is continuing abuse (physical, mental, emotional, or sexual) where you live, you may need further counseling help to deal with that situation.

If authorities abuse their position by requiring you to break God's law or compromise your commitment to Him, then you need to obey God rather than man. Be careful though. Don't assume that an authority is violating God's Word just because they are telling you to do something you don't like. We all need to adopt a humble, submissive spirit to one another in the fear of Christ. In addition, however, God has set up specific lines of authority to protect us and to give order to our daily lives. (Anderson, *The Bondage Breaker,* Chapter 4, pgs. 57–74)

It is actually reported that there is sexual immorality among you, and of a kind that does not occur even among pagans: A man has his father's wife. And you are proud! Shouldn't you rather have been filled with grief and have put out of your fellowship the man who did this? Even though I am not physically present, I am with you in spirit. And I have already passed judgment on the one who did this, just as if I were present. When you are assembled in the name of our Lord Jesus and I am with you in spirit, and the power of our Lord Jesus is present, hand this man over to Satan, so that the sinful nature may be destroyed and his spirit saved on the day of the Lord. Your boasting is not good. Don't you know that a little yeast works through the whole batch of dough? Get rid of the old yeast that you may be a new batch without yeast, as you really are. For Christ, our Passover lamb, has been sacrificed. Therefore let us keep the Festival, not with the old yeast, the yeast of malice and wickedness, but with bread without yeast, the bread of sincerity and truth. I have written you in my letter not to associate with sexually immoral people, not at all meaning the people of this world who are immoral, or the greedy and swindlers, or idolaters. In that case you would have to leave this world. But now I am writing you that you must not associate with anyone who calls himself a brother but

is sexually immoral or greedy, an idolater or a slanderer, a drunkard or a swindler. With such a man do not even eat. What business is it of mine to judge those outside the church? Are you not to judge those inside? God will judge those outside. "Expel the wicked man from among you."
I Corinthians 5:1–12

The term leaven is used here as a symbol of corruption of human nature. If an element of corruption is allowed to remain in the church, the whole church will become corrupted. "Hand this man over to Satan" means exclude him from fellowship, in hopes that left alone with sin and Satan, would motivate him to repentance (*Life Application Bible*, pg. 2068). Allowing and ignoring flagrant sin is harmful to all its members. We are not expected to be sinless, we are expected to encourage pray for and build one another up. However, we must be intolerant of sin that jeopardizes the spiritual health of a church. This is not talking about trivial sins and sinner but those sins that are without remorse.

Do you not know that your body is a temple of the Holy Spirit, who is in you, whom you have received from God? You are not your own; you were bought at a price. Therefore honor God with your body.
1 Corinthians 6:19

The Holy Spirit dwells within us, and in the deepest sense we are not our own. A great ransom was paid for us, and we are to glorify God in body and Spirit. Therefore, we are not free to do what we will with our bodies. The blood of Christ bought us.

Satan wants to chip away at us through our sinful nature and tell us that our bodies are our own.

Follow the way of love and eagerly desire spiritual gifts, especially the gift of prophecy. **1 Corinthians 14:1**

The one who has called us to warfare will equip us for warfare. We should earnestly desire the power gifts of the Holy Spirit. These gifts increase by faith and by use. (Hammond, *Demons and Deliverance*, pg. 21)

For he must reign until he has put all his enemies under his feet. **1 Corinthians 15:25**

Each person of the Trinity has work to do. The work of Christ was to conquer all evil on earth. He defeated sin and death on the cross and in the final days, he will defeat Satan and all evil. Paul carries our minds beyond the bounds of space and time to the final victory of Christ being all and in all.

If you forgive anyone, I also forgive him. And what I have forgiven–if there was anything to forgive–I have forgiven him in the sight of Christ for your sake, in order that Satan might not outwit us. For we are not unaware of his schemes. **2 Corinthians 2:10–11**

We need to forgive others so Satan cannot take advantage of us. We are commanded to get rid of all bitterness in our lives and forgive others as we have been forgiven. Ask God to bring to your mind the people you need to forgive by praying the following prayer out loud:

> *Dear heavenly Father, I thank You for the riches of Your kindness, forbearance, and patience toward me, knowing that Your kindness has led me to repentance. I confess that I have not shown that same kindness and patience toward those who have hurt me. Instead, I have held on to my anger, bitterness, and resentment toward them. Please bring to my mind all the people I need to forgive in order that I may do so now. In Jesus' name. Amen (Anderson, The Bondage Breaker, pg. 197)*

Often we hold things against ourselves, punishing ourselves for wrong choices we've made in the past. Forgiving yourself is accepting the truth that God has already forgiven you in Christ. If God forgives you, you can forgive yourself. People who want to forget all that was done to them will find they cannot do it. Don't put off forgiving those who have hurt you, hoping the pain will one day go away. Once you choose to forgive someone, *then* Christ can come and begin to heal you of your hurts. But the healing cannot begin until you first forgive.

Since God requires you to forgive, it is something you can do. Sometimes it is very hard to forgive someone because we naturally want revenge for the things we have suffered. Forgiveness seems to go against our sense of what is right and fair. So we hold on to our anger, punishing people over and over again in our minds for the pain they've cause us.

But we are told by God never to take our own revenge

(Romans 12:19). Let God deal with the person. Let him or her off your hook because as long as you refuse to forgive someone, you are still hooked to that person. You are still chained to your past, bound up in your bitterness. By forgiving, you let the other person off your hook, but he or she is not off God's hook. You must trust that God will deal with the person justly and fairly, something you simply cannot do.

"But you don't know how much this person hurt me!" you say. You're right. We don't, but Jesus does, and He tells you to forgive. Don't you see? Until you let go of your anger and hatred, the person is still hurting you. You can't turn back the clock and change the past, but you can be free from it. You can stop the pain, but there is only one way to do it, forgive.

Forgiveness is mainly a matter of obedience to God. God wants you to be free; there is no other way. Jesus took the *eternal* consequences of sin upon Himself. God "made Him who knew no sin to be sin on our behalf that we might become the righteousness of God in Him."

Remember, Jesus did not wait for those who were crucifying Him to apologize before He forgave them. Even while they mocked and jeered at Him, He prayed, "Father, forgive them; for they do not know what they are doing."

Make the hard choice to forgive even if you don't feel like it. Once you chose to forgive, Satan will have lost his power over you in that area and God's healing touch will be free to move. Freedom is what you will gain right now, not necessarily an immediate change in feelings. (Anderson, *The Bondage Breaker*, Chapter 4, pgs. 57–74)

Rather, we have renounced secret and shameful ways; we do not use deception, nor do we distort the word of God. On the contrary, by setting forth the truth plainly we command ourselves to every man's conscience in the sight of God. **2 Corinthians 4:2**

This passage helps us identify four of Satan's specialties that must be renounced and rejected by the believer in order to walk in victory: Secrecy, Shame, Deception, and Distortion of Scripture. Satan's plans toward us are always the anti-thesis of God's. Our Redeemer wants to loose us from the closets of secrecy and bring us to a spacious place of joy and freedom. Satan wants to keep us bound in secrecy where he can weigh us down in guilt, misery and shame. I am not suggesting standing up in from of the congregation and sharing all of our secrets. Please take note of the contrast between sharing general faults and weaknesses, and mistakes with others and confessing every detail of every sin to God.

Remember there is a distinct difference between God and humans. God can take it. He will always forgive. He promises to forget. Sometimes Christians can't take the details of our secret shames without stumbling over them. (Moore, *Praying God's Word*, pg. 72)

We must remember when we talk about Jesus, we are standing in His presence, and He hears every word. Proclaim the truth of God's Word. (*Life Application Bible*, pg. 2097)

Therefore we do not lose heart. Though outwardly we are wasting away, yet inwardly we are being renewed day by day. For our light and momentary troubles are achieving for us an eternal glory that far outweighs them

*all. So we fix our eyes not on what is seen, but on what is
unseen. For what is seen is temporary, but what is unseen
is eternal.* **2 Corinthians 4:16–18**

A central part of walking in the truth and rejecting deception is to deal with the fears that plague our lives. First Peter 5:8
says that our enemy, the devil, prowls around like a roaring lion,
seeking people to devour. Just as a lion's roar strikes terror in the
hearts of those who hear it, so Satan uses fear to try to paralyze
Christians. His intimidation tactics are designed to rob us of faith
in God and drive us to try to get our needs met through the world
or the flesh.

Fear weakens us, causes us to be self-centered, and clouds our
minds so that all we can think about is the thing that frightens us.
But fear can only control us if we let it.

God, however, does not want us to be mastered by anything,
including fear. Jesus Christ is to be our only Master. In order to
begin to experience, freedom from the bondage of fear and the
ability to walk by faith in God, pray the following prayer from
your heart:

*Dear heavenly Father, I confess to You that I have listened
to the devil's roar and have allowed fear to master me. I
have not always walked by faith in You but instead have
focused on my feelings and circumstances. Thank You
for forgiving me for my unbelief. Right now I renounce
the spirit of fear and affirm the truth that you have not
given me a spirit of fear but of power, love and a sound
mind. Lord, please reveal to my mind now all the fears
that have been controlling me so I can renounce them and
be free to walk by faith in You.
I thank You for the freedom You give me to walk by*

faith and not by fear. In Jesus' powerful name, I pray. Amen. (Anderson, The Bondage Breaker, Chapter 4, pgs. 57–74)

. . . that God was reconciling the world to himself in Christ, not counting men's sins against them. And he has committed to us the message of reconciliation. We are therefore Christ's ambassadors, as though God were making his appeal through us. We implore you on Christ's behalf: Be reconciled to God. God made him who had no sin to be sin for us, so that in him we might become the righteousness of God. **2 Corinthians 5:19–21**

Pride is the original sin of Lucifer. It sets one person or group against another. Satan's strategy is always to divide and conquer, but God has given us a ministry of reconciliation. Consider for a moment the work of Christ in breaking down the long-standing barrier of racial prejudice between Jew and Gentile:

For (Christ) is our peace, who has made the two one and has destroyed the barrier, the dividing wall of hostility, by abolishing in his flesh the law with its commandments and regulations. His purpose was to create in himself one new man out of the two, thus making peace, and in this one body to reconcile both of them to God through the cross, by which he put to death their hostility. He came and preached peace to you who were far away and peace to those who were near. For through him we both have access to the Father by the one Spirit.

Many times we deny that there is prejudice or bigotry in our hearts, yet "nothing in all creation is hidden from God's sight. Everything is uncovered and lay bare before the eyes of him to whom we must give account." The following is a prayer, asking God to shine His light upon your heart and reveal any area of proud prejudice:

> *Dear heavenly Father, I know that You love all people equally and that You do not show favoritism. You accept people from every nation who love You and do what is right. You do not judge them based on skin color, race, economic standing, ethnic background, gender, denominational preference, or any other worldly matter. I confess that I have too often prejudged others or regarded myself superior because of these things. I have not always been a minister of reconciliation but have been a proud agent of division through my attitudes, words, and deeds. I repent of all hateful bigotry and proud prejudice, and I ask You, Lord, to now reveal to my mind all the specific ways in which this form of pride has corrupted my heart and mind. In Jesus' name. Amen. (Anderson, The Bondage Breaker, Chapter 4, pgs. 57–74)*

The way is now open for us to enter into God's forgiveness. Christ was not made to be a sinner but to be sin. He bore the full penalty for the sin of the whole world. When we trust in Christ, we make an exchange, our sin for His righteousness. We are released from sin and reconciled to God. What power and Glory God has. He is infinitely more powerful than Satan. We can stand on His promises of protection.

> *for though we live in the world, we do not wage war as the world does. The weapons we fight with are not the*

weapons of the world. On the contrary, they have divine power to demolish strongholds. We demolish arguments and every pretension that sets itself up against the knowledge of God, and we take captive every thought to make it obedient to Christ. And we will be ready to punish every act of disobedience, once your obedience is complete. **2 Corinthians 10:3–5**

Arguments, bullying, and compulsion are the methods of natural hearts. Opinions must be examined in the light of knowledge of God and truth and cast down if false. Every thought is to be brought into captivity to the obedience of Christ. We must remember that we are in a war. The war against sin and Satan. God needs to command our thoughts and actions if we are to win and live for him.

Defense mechanisms are similar to what Paul calls strongholds. Fortresses or strongholds are thought patterns that were programmed into our minds when we learned to live our lives before we knew God. Our world views were shaped by the environment we were raised in. What was learned has to be unlearned. If we have been trained wrong, can we be untrained? If we believed a lie, can we renounce that lie and choose to believe the truth? Can our minds be reprogrammed? That is what repentance is: a change of mind. We can be transformed by the renewing of our minds. We can be transformed because we have the mind of Christ within us and because the Holy Spirit will lead us into all truth.

Don't think that Satan is no longer interested in manipulating our mind in order to accomplish his purposes. Satan's aim is to infiltrate our thoughts with his thoughts, to promote his lies. He knows if he can control our thoughts, he can begin to take control of our minds and actions. In this I am not saying that a demon or Satan can possess us, but he can manipulate us in this way. In

Greek the word thought is *noema*. In 2 Corinthians 2:10–11, the word schemes comes from the same root word. Satan can take advantage of those who will not forgive. (Anderson, *The Bondage Breaker*, Chapter 4, pgs. 57–74)

It is for freedom that Christ has set us free. Stand firm, then, and do not let yourselves be burdened again by a yoke of slavery. **Galatians 5:1**

This scripture brings before us a privilege, a danger, and a duty. Unbelievers sometimes take great pride in the title of free thinkers, yet it would seem that the only freedom they allow is the freedom for expressing ideas with which they sympathize.

It is Christ who breaks the fetters of the mind. The Christian should dare to think, to question, to doubt. Christian liberty is in danger from without and within. There are always those who desire to exercise undue influence over others. The body of Christ must beware of the possibility that the force of habit wears grooves that become deep ruts out of which we cannot stir.

Rituals, with living emotion when first attached to worship, become cherished, venerated and fossilized to a point that they become an unrelenting weight in worship. How many times in your church meetings or in worship have you heard the words: "But we've always done it this way." This thinking process puts a noose on the possibilities of new and creative ways to worship.

We are called to take a stand against all encroachments on our Christian freedoms. The freedom is given by Christ; but we are exhorted to maintain it. He fought to win it; we must fight to hold it. We owe to our descendants the duty of maintaining intact the traditions and faith that was passed down to us.

Christ died to set us free from sin and from a long list of laws and regulations. Christ came to set us free, not free to do whatever we want because that would lead us back into slavery to our selfish desires. Rather, thanks to Christ, we are now free and able to do what was impossible before, to live unselfishly. Those who appeal to their freedom so that they can have their own way or indulge their own desires are falling back into sin. But it is also wrong to put a burden of law keeping on Christians. We must stand against those who would enslave us with rules, methods, or special conditions for being saved or growing in Christ. (*Life Application Bible*, pg. 2124)

Once an area of darkness has been brought to the light of God's Word and repented of, don't look back. When a sin has been dealt with, know that the power of Jesus' blood covers it and the Lord refuses to remember it. Don't try to bring up past sins that have already been covered by the blood. (Avles, *Becoming a Prayer Warrior*, pg. 50)

So, I say, live by the Spirit, and you will not gratify the desires of the sinful nature. For the sinful nature desires what is contrary to the Spirit, and the Spirit what is contrary to the sinful nature. They are in conflict with each other, so that you do not do what you want. But if you are led by the Spirit, you are not under law.
Galatians 5:16–17

God's children are to "walk by the Spirit." In physical walking each new step we take depends on the previous step if we are to maintain our balance. So the metaphor Paul used here tells us we are to conduct our lives in complete dependence on the Spirit of God. (Lightner, *Angels, Satan, and Demons*, pg. 114)

Many of the sins mentioned in the "works of the flesh" are spiritual sins. Flesh means the entire nature, sense and reason. As children of God, we have the Holy Spirit in us as a source of new life; and so there arises in us that irreconcilable war. There are two forces within us, the Holy Spirit and our old sinful nature. These forces are not equal; the Holy Spirit is infinitely stronger (*Life Application Bible*, pg. 2125). But we must not rely on our own wisdom; we will make wrong choices. Ask for empowerment of the Holy Spirit as well as His guidance.

Do not get drunk on wine, which leads to debauchery. Instead, be filled with the Spirit. **Ephesians 5:18**

Paul contrasts getting drunk with wine, which produces a temporary high, to being filled with the Spirit, which produces lasting joy. In Christ, we have a better joy, higher and longer lasting, to cure our depression, monotony, or tension. Submit yourself daily to his leading and draw constantly on his power. (*Life Application Bible*, pg. 2139)

Scripture exhorts believers to "be filled with the Spirit." This means to be controlled by Him. We can never get more of the Holy Spirit than we receive at the time of salvation, but we can give Him more of ourselves. The negative side of the command in this verse is, "Do not be drunk with wine." When a person is drunk, he is under wine's control. Similarly, believers are to be controlled by the Holy Spirit. When they are, Satan and his army of demons are unable to get a foothold on them. (Lightner, *Angels, Satan, and Demons*, pg. 114)

Finally, be strong in the Lord and in his mighty power. Put on the full armor of God so that you can take your stand against the devil's schemes. For our struggles is not against flesh and blood, but against the rulers, against the authorities, against the powers of this dark world and against the spiritual forces of evil in the heavenly realms. Therefore put on the full armor of God, so that when the day of evil comes, you may be able to stand your ground, and after you have done everything, to stand. Stand firm then, with the belt of truth buckled around your waist, with the breastplate of righteousness in place, and with your feet fitted with the readiness that comes from the gospel of peace. In addition to all this, take up the shield of faith, with which you can extinguish all the flaming arrows of the evil one. Take the helmet of salvation and the sword of the Spirit, which is the word of God. And pray in the Spirit on all occasions with all kinds of prayers and requests. With this in mind, be alert and always keep on praying for all the saints. **Ephesians 6:10–18**

The key to victory in both natural and spiritual warfare is to clearly identify the enemy, and to understand his character and methods. Pride kills. Pride says, "I don't need God or anyone else's help. I can handle it by myself." Oh no, you can't! We absolutely need God, and we desperately need each other. The apostle Paul wisely wrote, "We worship in the Spirit of God and glory in Christ Jesus and put *no confidence in the flesh.*" That is a good definition of humility: putting no confidence in the flesh, that is in us, but, rather, being *"strong in the Lord, and in the strength of His might."* Humility is confidence properly placed in God.

Proverbs 3:5–7 expresses a similar thought: "Trust in the LORD with all your heart, and do not lean on your own understanding. In all your ways acknowledge Him, and He will make your paths straight. Do not be wise in your own eyes; fear the LORD and turn away from evil." Use the following prayer to express your commitment to living humbly before God:

> *Dear heavenly Father, You have said that pride goes before destruction and an arrogant spirit before stumbling. I confess that I have been thinking mainly of myself and not of others. I have not denied myself, picked up my cross daily, and followed You. As a result I have given ground to the devil in my life. I have sinned by believing I could be happy and successful on my own. I confess that I have placed my will before Yours, and I have centered my life around myself instead of You.*
>
> *I repent of my pride and selfishness and pray that all ground gained in my members by the enemies of the Lord Jesus Christ would be canceled. I choose to rely on the Holy Spirit's power and guidance so I will do nothing from selfishness or empty conceit. With humility of mind, I will regard others as more important than myself. And I choose to make You, Lord, the most important of all in my life. Please show me now all the specific ways in which I have lived my life in pride. Enable me through love to serve others and in honor to prefer others. I ask all of this in the gentle and humble name of Jesus, my Lord. Amen. (Anderson, The Bondage Breaker, pg. 200)*

To say that Christians cannot be affected by demons removes the church from the position of having an adequate answer and assisting those who are under attack. A current misconception or more accurate deception of Satan is that demons were active when Christ was on earth, but their activity has subsided. Christians who hold this view are not embracing the whole council of God in light of what His Word says, nor are they facing reality.

A second deception is what the early church called demonic activity, we now know to be mental illness. This kind of statement undermines the credibility of Scripture. Some problems are psychological and some are spiritual. These are also current deceptions. There is no inner conflict that doesn't include our spirit, our soul, our mind, and our body. All these are tied together. There is no time that is safe for taking off the armor of God.

The spirits we face are very structured, organized and disciplined. Satan is the commander and chief of the forces of darkness. The first level under Satan is a group called principalities and princes. The text of Daniel 10:13, the archangel Michael came against a prince of darkness that was blocking the messenger from God reaching Daniel. Doesn't this suggest that Satan has a prince over every nation? Under him are other princes who carry out the plans that Satan has against the political, educational and entertainment structures of that nation.

The next level is the powers. These are probably more numerous and somewhat less independent and powerful than the princes. Yet, their name suggests very powerful activities, which they address against believers.

The next level down is the rulers of darkness. These are the real workhorses for Satan. The final level of spiritual beings is called spiritual wickedness or wicked spirits. These were probably the demons so often mentioned during the earthly life of our Lord.

"Putting on the armor" is something done by prayer and the daily practice of faith. Daily we need to appropriate our provided armor and put on our spiritual dress to do battle. A very close, hard fought battle is always before us. Facing the battle without armor is unthinkable. As we equip ourselves with the whole armor of God, we will find ourselves meditating on this armor and using it many times a day.

It is a worshipful experience to meditate upon each piece of the armor provided for us by God. This is the whole armor of God. It is a complete, total provision of God, sufficient to equip us to stand against the very worst Satan can dish out (Bubeck, *The Adversary*, pg. 71–74).

The enemies of the soul are not earthly forces, nor beings on an equal level of man, but evil spirits. The human soul is open to subtle and violent attacks; we must fit ourselves to resist the assaults of the evil one. Be strong means to use the strength that Christians have through their union with Christ.

Demons are not "flesh and blood." We face a powerful army whose goal is to defeat Christ's church. As we believe in Christ, these become our enemies and they try everything possible to turn us away from God and back to sin. Satan is constantly battling against us, God has given us victory through Jesus Christ and the Holy Spirit and his armor surrounding us (*Living Application Bible*, pg. 2141). To withstand these attacks we must depend on God's strength. The whole body of the church must be armed, each and every individual. Our power comes from the Holy Spirit and the gates of hell cannot overcome it. Put on the full armor of God. In Chapter Twelve (XII) there are prayers, one for putting on the full armor of God.

The helmet of salvation is the first piece of equipment. All other equipment is useless without the knowledge and assurance of our salvation. We have a tendency to doubt our salvation at times. Be assured of your salvation. Romans 8:16 states: *"The Spirit of God itself bears witness with our spirits, that we are the children of God."*

The next piece is the breastplate of righteousness. This righteousness is given to all that by faith accept Jesus as Lord and Savior. Remember we are saints who sin. Confession is essential. Confession is not just saying "I'm sorry." To confess, *homologeo* in Greek, means to acknowledge and/or agree. Therefore, to confess means to say, "I did it."

The third piece of armor is the shield of faith. There were two shields used by the Romans. The first was a narrow disc and of little value for protection. The second was literally a door, large enough to cover the whole person. This is the faith that will withstand the darts of our adversaries. The more we know about God and His Word, the more faith we will have. The less we know the smaller our shield will be.

The fourth piece of armor is the Sword of the Spirit. The Word of God is the only offensive weapon in this armor. The Greek word used here is *rhema* rather than *logos* in order to emphasize the spoken Word of God. The Greek word *rhema* brings in the idea of proclamation. Therefore, our defense against direct attacks by the devil is to speak aloud God's truth.

The fifth piece of armor are the shoes of peace. To wear the shoes of peace means we are to be peacemakers. Peacemakers bring people together and encourage reconciliation.

Last, is the girdle of truth. The girdle binds all the pieces together and is the Word of God. Christ is in us therefore, truth is in us. The belt of truth is our defense against Satan's primary weapon . . . deception. We all lie, but we need to remember that truth is never an enemy, it is a liberating friend. Facing the truth is the first step in any recovery program, and is necessary in all aspects of our mind, body, soul, emotions and spirit.

> *. . . being confident in this, that he who began a good work in you will carry it on to completion until the day of Christ Jesus.* **Philippians 1:6**

Sometimes we wonder if we are growing spiritually. We must remember when God begins something he finishes it. God will not give up on us.

> *And the peace of God which transcends all understanding will guard your hearts and your minds in Christ Jesus. Finally, brothers, whatever is true, whatever is noble, whatever is right, whatever is pure, whatever is lovely, whatever is admirable, if anything is excellent or praiseworthy, think about such things.*
> **Philippians 4:7–8**

How do we know whether those negative, lying, and condemning thoughts are from the evil one or are just our own flesh patterns? In one sense it doesn't make any difference. We are to take every thought captive to the obedience of Christ; that is, if it isn't true, don't believe it. Pray the prayer included in Chapter Twelve (XII) and ask God to guide you. Old patterns of thought don't just leave. They are slowly replaced or overcome as we renew our minds.

What is in our minds and hearts comes out in words and actions. We need to program our minds. We know we have trouble with impure thoughts. Read God's word and pray. It takes practice in focusing your mind but God can help us do it.

When you were dead in your sins and in the uncircumcision of your sinful nature, God made you alive with Christ. He forgave us all our sins, having canceled the written code, with its regulations, that was against us and that stood opposed to us; he took it away, nailing it to the cross. And having disarmed the powers and authorities, he made a public spectacle of them, triumphing over them by the cross. **Colossians 2:13–15**

Forgiveness is the great initial blessing bestowed upon us by Christ. Therefore, we have no powers to fear. We are no longer submitted to bondage, whether of the law or of angelic powers. Angelic powers refer to the devil and demons. We have a new nature. God crucified the old nature and replaced it with a loving nature. We are no longer under the power of sin. However, God does not take us out of a sinful world. We still feel like sinning. Sometimes we do commit sins. The difference is we are no longer slaves to sin, now we are free to live for Christ (*Life Application Bible*, pg. 2163). The Holy Spirit helps us. We need to work at remembering we have victory in Jesus.

———————

Since, then, you have been raised with Christ, set your hearts on things above, where Christ is seated at the right hand of God. Set your minds on things above, not on earthly things. For you died, and your life is now hidden with Christ in God. When Christ, who is your life, appears, then you also will appear with him in glory. Put to death, therefore, whatever belongs to your earthly nature; sexual immorality, impurity, lust, evil desires, and greed, which is idolatry. Because of these, the wrath

> *of God is coming. You used to walk in these ways, in the life you once lived. But now you must rid yourselves of all such things as these: anger, rage, malice, slander, and filthy language from your lips. Do not lie to each other, since you have taken off your old self with its practices and have put on the new self, which is being renewed in knowledge in the image of its Creator. Here there is no Greek or Jew, circumcised or uncircumcised, barbarian, Scythian, slave or free, but Christ is all, and is in all. Therefore, as God's chosen people, holy and dearly loved, clothe yourself with compassion, kindness, humility, gentleness and patience. Bear with each other and forgive whatever grievances you may have against one another. Forgive as the Lord forgave you. And over all these virtues put on love, which binds them all together in perfect unity. Let the peace of Christ rule in your hearts, since as members of one body you were called to peace. And be thankful.*

Colossians 3:2–15

When a believer is "hidden with Christ" they are concealed and safe. The more we know of Christ, the more we are charged to be like him (*Life Application Bible*, pg. 2166). To live in Christ daily we attempt to imitate His compassion and forgiving attitude, let love guide our lives, let the peace of Christ rule our hearts, be thankful and keep God's Word in our hearts.

> *Be joyful always; pray continually; give thanks in all circumstances, for this is God's will for you in Christ Jesus. Do not put out the Spirit's fire; do not treat prophecies*

with contempt. Test everything. Hold on to the good.
Avoid every kind of evil. **1 Thessalonians 5:16–22**

Believers are not to "quench the Spirit." To quench means to suppress or stifle. We do this to the indwelling Holy Spirit when we say no to His ministry to our hearts. In other words, sin quenches the Spirit; it stifles His work in and through us. (Lightner, *Angels, Satan, and Demons*, pg. 114)

"Watch and pray," should be engraved on the shield of every Christian warrior. We are exhorted to lead orderly and peaceable lives, active in well doing. Christian life is to be lived in an atmosphere of continual joy, prayer and gratitude to God. Do not quench the Spirit. By this I mean do not ignore or put aside the gifts of the Holy Spirit. Do not smother your gifts. Thank God IN everything not FOR everything. Evil does not come from God, so don't give thanks for it, but thank God for His presence and for the strength He gives. Obey these three commands: be joyous, pray continually, and give thanks (*Life Application Bible*, pg. 2176). Have a prayerful attitude.

Finally, brothers, pray for us that the message of the Lord may spread rapidly and be honored, just as it was with you. And pray that we may be delivered from wicked and evil men, for not everyone has faith. But the Lord is faithful and he will strengthen and protect you from the evil one. We have confidence in the Lord that you are doing and will continue to do the things we command. May the Lord direct your hearts into God's love and Christ's perseverance. **2 Thessalonians 3:1–5**

Beneath the surface of daily life, a spiritual battle is being waged. Our primary defense is prayer invoking the power of God to protect and strengthen us. How do we prepare for these satanic attacks? Take the threat of Satan seriously, pray for strength, study scripture, memorize scripture so that you take it with you, associate with those who speak the truth and practice what you are taught (*Life Application Bible*, pg. 2183).

> *Timothy, my son, I give you this instruction in keeping with the prophecies once made about you, so that by following them you may fight the good fight, holding on to faith and a good conscience. Some have rejected these and so have shipwrecked their faith. Among them are Hymenaeus and Alexander, whom I have handed over to Satan to be taught not to blaspheme.*
> **1 Timothy 1:18–20**

Treasure your faith more than anything else. Listen to your conscience, to ignore it is to harden your heart. Eventually you will not know how to discern wrong and right (*Life Application Bible*, pg. 2188). Again, here is the mention of turning someone over to Satan to motivate toward repentance. Pray for each other and for our leaders, prayer has powerful results.

> *That is why I am suffering as I am. Yet I am not ashamed, because I know whom I have believed, and am convinced that he is able to guard what I have entrusted to him for that day.* **2 Timothy 1:12**

Paul was in prison, but that did not stop his ministry. He trusted God to use him regardless of his circumstances. If your situation looks bleak, give your concerns to Christ. He will guard your faith. (*Life Application Bible*, pg. 2199)

We should trust God regardless of our circumstances. If the situation looks bleak, give the concerns to Christ. He will guard your faith.

Flee the evil desires of youth, and pursue righteousness, faith, love and peace, along with those who call on the Lord out of a pure heart. Don't have anything to do with foolish and stupid arguments, because you know they produce quarrels. And the Lord's servant must not quarrel; instead, he must be kind to everyone, able to teach, not resentful. Those who oppose him he must gently instruct, in the hope that God will grant them repentance leading them to a knowledge of the truth, and that they will come to their senses and escape from the trap of the devil, who has taken them captive to do his will.

2 Timothy 2:22–26

God's Word is true and we need to accept His truth in the innermost part of our being. Whether or not we *feel* it is true, we need to *believe* it is true! Since Jesus is the truth, the Holy Spirit is the Spirit of truth, and the Word of God is truth, we ought to speak the truth in love.

The believer in Christ has no business deceiving others by lying, telling "white" lies, exaggerating, stretching the truth, or anything related to falsehoods. Satan is the father of lies, and he seeks to keep people in bondage through deception, but it is the truth in Jesus that sets us free. We will find real joy and freedom when we stop living a lie and walk openly in the truth. After confessing his sin, King David wrote, "How blessed (Happy) is the man . . . in whose spirit there is no deceit!" (Psalm 32:2) (Anderson, *The Steps to Freedom in Christ*, pg. 5)

Defilement from within, as well as from without, must be avoided, and fellowship with the sincere is to be pursued. Running away is sometimes considered cowardly (*Life Application Bible*, pg. 2202). However, wise people realize that removing themselves physically from temptation can be the most courageous action to take. Knowing when to run is as important in spiritual battle as knowing when and how to fight.

In the presence of God and Christ Jesus, who will judge the living and the dead, and in view of his appearing and his kingdom, I give you this charge: Preach the Word; be prepared in season and out of season; correct, rebuke and encourage—with great patience and careful instruction. For the time will come when men will not put up with sound doctrine. Instead, to suit their own desires, they will gather around them a great number of teachers to say what their itching ears want to hear. They will turn their ears away from the truth and turn aside to myths. But you, keep your head in all situations, endure hardship, do the work of an evangelist, discharge all the duties of your ministry. 2 Timothy 4:1–5

"Be prepared in season and out of season" means to always be ready to serve God in any situation. Be sensitive to the opportunities God gives you. Paul told Timothy to "Correct, rebuke and encourage." It is difficult to accept correction, to be told we have to change. But no matter how much the truth hurts, we must be willing to listen to it so we can more fully obey God. (*Life Application Bible*, pg. 2203) Underline the word reprove in your Bible. The word reprove means "to prove again" from the source. Our source is the Scriptures. (Renner, *Seducing Spirits and Doctrine of Demons*, pg. 73)

You must teach what is in accord with sound doctrine. Teach the older men to be temperate, worthy of respect, self-controlled, and sound in faith, in love and in endurance. Likewise, teach the older women to be reverent in the way they live, not to be slanderers or addicted to much wine, but to teach what is good. Then they can train the younger women to love their husbands and children, to be self-controlled and pure, to be busy at home, to be kind, and to be subject to their husbands, so that no one will malign the word of God. Similarly, encourage the young men to be self-controlled. In everything set them an example by doing what is good. In your teaching show integrity, seriousness and soundness of speech that cannot be condemned, so that those who oppose you may be ashamed because they have nothing bad to say about us. Teach slaves to be subject to their masters in everything, to try to please them, not to talk back to them, and not to steal from them, but to show that they can be fully trusted, so that in every way they will make the teaching about God our Savior attractive. For the grace of God that brings salvation has appeared to all men. It teaches us to say "No' to ungodliness and worldly passions, and to live

> *self-controlled, upright and godly lives in the present age,*
> *while we wait for the blessed hope, the glorious appearing*
> *of our great God and Savior, Jesus Christ, who gave*
> *himself for us to redeem us from all wickedness and to*
> *purify for himself a people that are his very own, eager*
> *to do what is good. These, then, are the things you should*
> *teach. Encourage and rebuke with all authority. Do not*
> *let anyone despise you.* **Titus 2:1–15**

Verses 11–14 are notable for their perfect balance of doctrine and living. Beginning with incarnation (which means the grace of God has appeared) they relate this doctrine to a life that denies evil and practices good here and now, that sees in the return of Christ the incentive for godly conduct (looking for the blessed hope) and that realizes, in personal holiness and good works, the purpose of atonement. (*New Scofield Bible*, pg. 1710)

The best antidote to wrong teaching is positive moral exhortation and teaching which promotes spiritual health. Those who follow wrong teachings are first corrupt in heart, and then the corruption of action follows. Therefore, those who desire by their teaching to maintain the true spiritual well being of others must demand the consistent action of heart soundness. There are two doctrines of the gospels listed here, sanctification and righteousness, both of which are directed to show that a life of good works is God's purpose and the only appropriate behavior for all who enjoy the benefits of Christ's redeeming grace and saving mercy. Foolish inquires and subjects, which are products that create strife and division, should be avoided.

Notice the emphasis on "Sound doctrine." This is the content of our faith. Believers must be grounded in the truths of the Bible. We need to teach and live by example the truths in scripture. The power to live as a Christian comes from the Holy Spirit. Because

Christ died and rescued us from sin, we are free from sin's control. God gives us the power and understanding to live according to his will and to do good. Then we will look forward to Christ's wonderful return with eager expectation and hope.

It is not enough to renounce sin and evil desires; we must also live actively for God. To fight against lust we must say no to temptation, but we must also say yes to active service for Christ. Christ's redeeming us opens the way for him to purify us. Redeem means to purchase our release from the captivity of sin with a ransom. We are not only free from the sentence of death for our sin, but we are also purified from sin's influence as we grow in Christ (*Life Application Bible*, pg. 2210).

The question here is do we assist each other in this basic function. Do we, as "adults" in faith, truly pass sound doctrine and sound lives to the younger people in our church? We must master our wills, our tongues, and our passions so that Christ will not be dishonored. How is our self-control? Do not let the seriousness of the gospel cause us to repel others by our grim disposition. If we are impulsive, unreasonable, and confusing, we are likely to block the work of the Holy Spirit in those around us rather than plant a seed of truth. God gives us the power and understanding to live according to his will.

Since the children have flesh and blood, he too shared in their humanity so that by his death he might destroy him who holds the power of death, that is, the devil, and free those who all their lives were held in slavery by their fear of death. **Hebrews 2:14–15**

The purpose of the incarnation, in understanding the account given here, we must remember that death, originally announced as the penalty of transgression, is regarded in the New Testament as the sign of the continual dominion of sin over the human race. "Having the power of death or dominion over" means that Satan has had the dominion over death allowed him because of human sin. Christ's death has not as yet abolished death itself; only to have rendered Satan impotent; for natural death still occurs, though to believers it has no sting.

We as sinners are subject to bondage and fear, held under by the devil and the power of death. The bondage and hold on us of the devil has been broken. This was done when the Son of God became human, entered into death, not as a victim, but as the decisive victor over death and Satan. We belong to God; therefore, we need not fear death, because we know it is only the doorway to eternal life. Victory through the blood of Jesus Christ.

For the word of God is living and active. Sharper than any double edged sword, it penetrates even to dividing soul and spirit, joints and morrow; it judges the thoughts and attitudes of the heart. Nothing in all creation is hidden from God's sight. Everything is uncovered and laid bare before the eyes of him to whom we must give account. **Hebrews 4:12–13**

How can a young man or woman keep their way pure? By living according to your word. I seek you with all my heart; do not let me stray from your commands. I have hidden your word in my heart that I might no sin against you. **Psalm 119:9–11**

*I have given you authority to trample on snakes, scorpions
and to overcome all the power of the enemy; nothing will
harm you.* **Luke 10:19**

The Word of God is not simply a collection of words from
God, a vehicle for communicating ideas; it is living, life-changing
and dynamic as it works in us. With the incisiveness of a surgeon's
knife, God's Word reveals who we are and what we are not. It
penetrates the core of our moral and spiritual life. It discerns what
is within us, both good and evil. The demands of God's Word
requires a decision, to let it shape our lives.

Nothing can be hidden from God. He knows about everyone,
everywhere, and everything about us is wide open to His all-see-
ing eyes. God sees all we do and knows all we think. Even when
we are unaware of His presence, He is there. When we try to hide
from him, He sees us. We have no secrets from God. It's comforting to know that although God knows us intimately, He still loves
us. (*Life Application Bible*, pg. 2224)

We are drowning in a sea of impurity. Everywhere we look we
find temptations. How do we stay pure in a filthy environment?
We cannot do this on our own. Where can we find strength and
wisdom? By reading God's Word and doing what it says. Hiding
God's word in our hearts is the best deterrent to sin, if we use it as
a guide for everything we do. (*Life Application Bible*, pg. 1036)

We cannot hide our mental sins from God because He knows
our hearts and minds, even if no one else knows about them. Once
we act on those thoughts, no matter how secret, we cannot hide
our sin from God or from Satan. When we sin we give Satan the
legal right to attack and defeat us. It is for this reason we must
know the Word of God. *How can a young man keep his way pure?
By living according to your word. I seek you with all my heart; do
not let me stray from your commands. I have hidden your word in my*

heart that I might not sin against you (Psalm 119:9–11). Jesus tells us in Luke 10:19, Mark 16:17, and 2 Corinthians 7:1 that he was giving us authority over Satan and his kingdom. With authority comes responsibility. It is our responsibility to break any curses on us. Jesus gave us the power and he expects us to use this power in His name. (Anderson, *The Bondage Breaker*, Chapter 5, pgs. 75–94)

> *Do not merely listen to the word, and so deceive yourselves. Do what it says. Anyone who listens to the word but does not do what it says is like a man who looks at his face in a mirror and, after looking at himself, goes away and immediately forgets what he looks like. But the man who looks intently into the perfect law that gives freedom, and continues to do this, not forgetting what he has heard, but doing it (ginomai), he will be blessed in what he does.*
> **James 1:22–25**

When we first hear this verse we become overwhelmed by it, we think we have to instantly, overnight, be accountable for the entire world. We have to become instantly perfect, without blemish, fault, or sin. But the Greek word *ginomai* means be yourself becoming a doer of the word. In other words, start where we are. It's time to develop into who God wants us to be. (Renner, *Seducing Spirits and Doctrines of Demons*, pg. 111) We can measure the effectiveness of our Bible study time by the effect it has on our behavior and attitudes. It seems paradoxical that a law could give us freedom, but God's law points out sin in us and gives us the opportunity to ask for God's forgiveness. As Christians, we are saved by God's grace, and salvation frees us from sin's control. (*Life Application Bible*, pg. 2246)

The tongue also is a fire, a world of evil among the parts of the body. It corrupts the whole person, sets the whole course of his life on fire, and is itself set on fire by hell. All kinds of animals, birds, reptiles and creatures of the sea are being tamed and have been tamed by man, but no man can tame the tongue. It is restless evil, full of deadly poison. With the tongue we praise our Lord and Father, and with it we curse men, who have been made in God's likeness. Out of the same mouth come praise and cursing. My brothers and sisters, this should not be. Can both fresh water and salt water flow from the same spring? My brothers, can a fig tree bear olives, or a grapevine bear figs? Neither can a salt spring produce fresh water.

James 3:6–12

James compares the damage the tongue can do to a raging fire; the tongue's wickedness has its source in hell itself. The uncontrolled tongue can do terrible damage. Satan uses the tongue to divide people and put them against one another. Talk and hateful words are damaging because they spread destruction quickly and no one can stop the results once they are spoken. We dare not be careless with what we say, thinking we can apologize later, because even if we do, the scar remains. A few words spoken in anger can destroy a relationship that took years to build. Before you speak, remember that words are like fire; you can neither control nor reverse the damage they do.

If no human being can control the tongue, why bother trying?

Even if we may not achieve perfect control of our tongues, we can still learn enough control to reduce the damage our words can do. It is better to fight a fire than to go around setting new ones. Remember that we are not fighting the tongue's fire in our own strength. The Holy Spirit will give us increasing power to monitor and control what we say, so that when we are offended, the Spirit will remind us of God's love, and we won't react in a hateful manner. When we are criticized, the Spirit will heal the hurt, and we won't lash out.

Be careful about making negative and hurtful statements. God holds us directly responsible for every word we say. Hate in God's eyes is the same as murder. Our words and/or hatred becomes a curse. This Scripture emphasizes how evil can be sent through spoken words.

Our contradictory speech often puzzles us. At times our words are right and pleasing to God, but at other times they are violent and destructive. Which of these speech patterns reflects our true identity? The tongue gives us a picture of our basic human nature. We were made in God's image, but we have also fallen into sin. God works to change us from the inside out. When the Holy Spirit purifies our hearts, he gives self-control so that the person will speak words that please God. (*Life Application Bible*, pg. 2248)

Submit yourselves, then, to God. Resist the devil, and he will flee from you. Come near to God and he will come near to you. Wash your hands, you sinners, and purify your hearts, you double-minded. Come near to God and he will come near to you. Wash your hands, you sinners, and purify your hearts, you double-minded. Grieve, mourn and wail. Change your laughter to mourning and your joy to gloom. Humble yourselves before the Lord, and he will lift you up. **James 4:7–10**

These verses in James 4 include ten commands. In Greek, each one is an aorist imperative, stressing the need for decisive action on the part of believers. The command to "resist the devil" follows the command to "submit therefore to God." "Submit" is a military term meaning to be subordinated, that is, to give obedience to one's superior. This is the positive side. The negative side is to "resist," that is, stand against or oppose the devil. When believers carry out their responsibilities, God promises that the devil "will flee from you." (Lightner, *Angels, Satan, and Demons*, pg. 160)

Many times we feel trapped in a vicious cycle of "sin-confess-sin-confess" that never seems to end. We can become very discouraged and end up just giving up and giving in to the sins of our flesh. To find freedom we must follow James 4:7, "Submit therefore to God. Resist the devil and he will flee from you." We submit to God by confession of sin and repentance. We resist the devil by rejecting his lies. Instead, we walk in the truth and put on the full armor of God.

Sin that has become a habit often requires help from a trusted brother or sister in Christ. James 5:16 says, "Confess your sins to one another, and pray for one another, so that you may be healed. The effective prayer of a righteous man can accomplish much." Sometimes the assurance of 1 John 1:9 is enough: "If we confess our sins, He is faithful and righteous to forgive us our sins and to cleanse us from all unrighteousness."

Remember, confession is not saying, "I'm sorry"; it is openly admitting, "I did it." Whether you need help from other people or just the accountability of walking in the light before God, pray the following prayer out loud:

Dear heavenly Father, You have told me to put on the Lord Jesus Christ and make no provision for the flesh in regard to its lust. I confess that I have given in to fleshly lusts that wage war against my soul. I thank You that in Christ my sins are already forgiven, but I have broken Your holy law and given the devil a chance to wage war in my body. I come to You now to confess and renounce these sins of the flesh so that I might be cleansed and set free from the bondage of sin. Please reveal to my mind now all the sins of the flesh I have committed and the ways I have grieved the Holy Spirit. In Jesus' holy name, I pray. Amen (Anderson. The Bondage Breaker, pg. 202)

What is the abiding secret of victory in the war against worldliness and sin? It consists of two activities, submission to God and resistance to the devil. By faith, we submit to God in a fuller and deeper surrender to His will, this means complete submission of self, will, family, possessions, everything to God (Rogerson, *The Angels of God*, handout). In submission, we are prepared for conflict with the evil one; and at the same time our powers of resistance are strengthened and multiplied. God never refuses to meet us as we sincerely seek His face. There is more involved in drawing near to God than just in prayer. It means growing in our close walk of fellowship with God and in demands fitting preparation. With the power of the Holy Spirit, we can resist the devil, and he will flee from us. The authority of the devil is not equal to the authority of God. The believer has no authority, only God and Christ have authority. The believer is protected through their relationship with Christ by the authority of God (Rogerson, *The Angels of God*, handout). We are warned against being double minded which means that we are not to strive to maintain a loyalty to the Lord and an allegiance to the world. We cannot have both.

Therefore, prepare your minds for action; be self-controlled; set your hope fully on the grace to be given you when Jesus Christ is revealed. **1 Peter 1:13**

Other translations have "gird up" which means to bind up the loose flowing robes which hamper freedom of movement. It is a call to attitude. The loins are the mind in the scripture. We are summoned to strenuous thinking so that we might understand, and be able to exercise an intelligent faith. To be sober is more than avoiding drunkenness. It means seriousness and alertness in thought and conduct. Stay mentally alert and focused. We need to prepare our minds for action by discipline of prayer, study and worship.

For you know that it was not with perishable things such as silver or gold that you were redeemed from the empty way of life handed down to you from your forefathers, but with the precious blood of Christ, a lamb without blemish or defect. **1 Peter 1:18–19**

To redeem means to release by paying a ransom price. The Greek word *diamonizomai* is translated as: to be under the power of a demon. There is a vast difference between being possessed, i.e., owned, by demons and being influenced by demons. Alex Konya has well summarized the New Testament teaching on the meaning of demon possession: It is "The invasion of a victim's body by a demon (or demons), in which the demon exercises living and sovereign control over the victim, which the victim cannot successfully resist." (Konya, *Demons: A Biblical Based Perspective*, pg. 22)

Demonic influence describes the general work of demons against God and His people. It is both constant and continuous. Merrill F. Unger draws distinctions between demon influence and demon possession in this way: "In demon influence, evil spirits exert power over a person short of actual possession. Such influence may vary from mild harassment to extreme subjection when body and mind become dominated and are held in slavery by spirit agents. Christians as well as non-Christians can be so influenced. They may be oppressed, vexed, depressed, hindered, and bound by demons. (Unger, *Demons in the World Today*, pg. 113)

The question that faces us is; can property owned by one person be trespassed upon by another person? Suppose a landowner has a wooded piece of property that affords good squirrel hunting. A trespasser can come upon that property and begin to shoot squirrels; he can be put off the property as one who has no legal rights. This is precisely what takes place when a demon tries to indwell a Christian. The evil spirit has no rights of ownership. Therefore, when the evil spirit is commanded to go, by his owner or His representative of authority, the evil spirit has no choice but to go. (Hammond, *Demons and Deliverance*, pgs. 15–16)

A slave was redeemed when someone paid money to buy his freedom. God redeemed us from the tyranny of sin, not with money, but with the precious blood of his own Son. We cannot escape from sin on our own; only the life and blood of God's Son can free us. (*Life Application Bible*, pg. 2258)

Like newborn babies, crave pure spiritual milk, so that by it you may grow up in your salvation, now that you have tasted that the Lord is good. 1 Peter 2:2

The "pure milk" is God's Word and enables us to "grow in respect to salvation." Conviction of sin comes about through the Word. God's Word convicts the believer of sin. It serves as a mirror, showing us our need (James 1:23–24). It is "able to judge the thoughts and intentions of the heart" (Hebrews 4:12). Scripture provides cleansing for the child of God (John 15:3). Christ cleanses the church through the Word (Ephesians 5:25–26). Guidance for the pilgrim-believer is found in God's Word (Psalm 40:8). The Word arms the believer against temptation. It is the "sword of the Spirit" by which the believer is to do battle with Satan (Ephesians 6:17). Through God's Word we are made sensitive to Satan and his vicious ways, because God's Word "is a lamp to our feet (Psalm 119:105). The Word of God is used by the Spirit of God to equip God's people for service (2 Timothy 3:16–17).

However, the Bible is not a good luck charm. It is not through the process of osmosis that these essentials for effective Christian living and service come to Christians. God's Word must be digested spiritually, just as food we eat must be digested if it is to provide nourishment for our bodies. Therefore we need to read God's Word regularly (Acts 17:11), systematically (2 Timothy 2:15), prayerfully (Psalm 119:125), attentively (Psalm 199:131), and obediently (John 15:10), and to know it thoroughly (2 Timothy 3:15; Jeremiah 15:16). (Lightner, *Angels, Satan, and Demons*, pg. 115)

We must remember that the one characteristic all children share is that they want to grow up to be like big brothers, sisters or parents. When we are born again, we become spiritual newborn babies. If we are healthy, we will yearn to grow. The need for milk is a natural instinct for a baby, and it signals the desire for nourishment that will lead to growth. Once we see our need for God's Word and begin to find nourishment in Christ, our spiritual appetite will increase and we will start to mature. How strong is our desire for God's Word? (Life Application Bible, pg. 2259)

Dear friends, do not be surprised at the painful trial you are suffering, as though something strange was happening to you. But rejoice that you participate in the sufferings of Christ, so that you may be overjoyed when his glory is revealed. **1 Peter 4:12–13**

Notice in earlier scripture how Jesus prayed for Peter. He prayed that his faith would not fail. It is the shield of faith which quenches all the fiery darts of the evil one. Fear is a fiery dart that only faith can quench. Fear is defeated by faith. We can have lapses of faith, which is different from total failures of faith. Peter was sustained by the intercession of Jesus from complete disaster. It is comforting to realize that Jesus intercedes for each of us personally. Peter is telling us that we are not unlike him in our struggles and lapses of faith, fear or doubt. (Hammond, *Demons and Deliverance*, pg. 136)

This is the message we have heard from him and declare to you: God is light; in him there is no darkness at all. If we claim to have fellowship with him yet walk in the darkness, we lie and do not live by the truth. But if we walk in the light, as he is in the light, we have fellowship

with one another, and the blood of Jesus, his Son, purifies
us from all sin. If we claim to be without sin, we deceive
ourselves and the truth is not in us. If we confess our sins,
he is faithful and just and will forgive us our sins, and
purify us from all unrighteousness. If we claim we have
not sinned, we make him out to be a liar and his word has
no place in our lives. **1 John 1:5–9**

How can we find the strength to walk in the light? When we are sure God loves and accepts us, we can be free to own up to our sins and face reality instead of running and hiding from painful circumstances.

Start this step by praying the following prayer out loud. Don't let any opposing thoughts, such as, "This is a waste of time" or "I wish I could believe this stuff but I just can't," keep you from praying and choosing the truth. Even if this is difficult for you, work your way through this step. God will strengthen you as you rely on Him.

> *Dear heavenly Father, I know that You want me to*
> *know the truth, believe the truth, and speak the truth.*
> *Thank You that it is the truth that will set me free. In*
> *many ways I have been deceived by Satan, the father of*
> *lies, and I have deceived myself as well.*
>
> *Father, I pray in the name of the Lord Jesus Christ, by*
> *virtue of His shed blood and resurrection, asking You to*
> *rebuke all of Satan's demons that are deceiving me.*
>
> *I have trusted in Jesus alone to save me, and so I am Your*
> *forgiven child. Therefore, since You accept me just as I*
> *am in Christ, I can be free to face my sin and not try to*
> *hide. I ask for the Holy Spirit to guide me into all truth.*
> *I ask You to "search me, O God, and know my heart; try*

> *me and know my anxious thought, and see if there be any*
> *hurtful way in me, and lead me in the everlasting way.""*
> *In the name of Jesus, who is the Truth, I pray, Amen.*
> *(Anderson, The Steps to Freedom in Christ, pg. 5)*

Through the Word of God, the indwelling Holy Spirit shows the Christian that we still possess an old nature and need forgiveness for our sins. The blood of Christ is the divine provision for both. To walk in the light is to live in fellowship with the Father and the Son. Sin interrupts fellowship but cannot change the relationship. Confession restores fellowship and immediate confession keeps the fellowship unbroken. (*New Scofield Bible*, pg. 1756)

John claims three obstacles to fellowship with God. First, there is the allegation that we have fellowship with Christ while we walk in darkness. This is a lie, for since God is light it is not possible to be in fellowship with Him and the same time to be in darkness. Light and darkness are incompatible. The second false teaching is that we have no sin. We might compare the person today who says that sin doesn't exist only diseases, or weakness, or heredity, environment, necessity or the like so that it is fate but not their fault. This person deceives himself or herself. By contrast, if we confess our sins, we receive forgiveness. The third error is to say we have not sinned. This claim of spinelessness calls God a liar, because the whole of God's dealings with mankind implies our need for forgiveness and salvation (*Life Application Bible*, pg. 2275).

False teachers say we have no natural tendency toward sin, and that once we are saved we were then incapable of sinning. Sin does exist and even after being saved, we still need to confess our sins. We must take sin seriously.

He who does what is sinful is of the devil, because the devil has been sinning from the beginning. The reason the Son of God appeared was to destroy the devil's work. No one who is born of God will continue to sin, because God's seed remains in him; he cannot go on sinning, because he has been born of God. **1 John 3:8–9**

In this Epistle, the verb "is" has the force of a continuous present tense and thus denotes a person's habitual attitude toward sin as expressed in participation in sin. John is not speaking of a state of perfection in which it is impossible for a Christian ever to attain; but he is stressing the fact that a Christian cannot keep on practicing sin, because he is re-born.

"Righteousness" here means the righteous life which is the result of salvation through Christ. By God's grace the Christian does righteously because he has been made righteous. (*New Schofield Bible*, pg. 1758)

Lawlessness is the assertion of the individual will against and in defiance of the law of God, the refusal to live in accordance with the revealed standards of right and wrong. As children of God, this attitude should be alien to us. We must remember the purpose for which Jesus came into the world to take away our sin, and to destroy the works of the devil. "Whosoever abides in Him does not sin; he cannot sin, because he is born of God." This statement should not be watered down. We must never grow complacent in our attitude towards sin, even occasional sin.

The life we lead reveals the source from which we draw our life. If we are born again from above, we will habitually lead the life of a born again person, in spite of stumbles; if we continually sin, we are of the devil. False teachers are wrong in saying sin does not matter. Life is a test; if we are Christ's we shall be Christ like.

We all have areas where the temptation is strong and habits are hard to break. These areas give the devil a foothold, so we must look closely at our areas of vulnerability. If we are struggling with a particular habit and are truly working at conquering that habit for Christ then this verse is not talking about that particular sin (*Life Application Bible*, pg. 2279). John is not talking about those whose victory over a particular sin is not complete, but to those who make a practice of sinning and look for ways to justify that sin. There are three steps to victory over continuing control of a particular sin; seek the power of the Holy Spirit and God's Word; stay away from tempting situations; seek the help of the body of Christ. We should work towards being open to the community of faith in their willingness to hold us accountable.

> *Dear friends, do not believe every spirit, but test the spirits to see whether they are from God, because many false prophets have gone out into the world. This is how you can recognize the Spirit of God: Every spirit that acknowledges that Jesus Christ has come in the flesh is from God, but every spirit that does not acknowledge Jesus is not from God. This is the spirit of the antichrist, which you have heard, is coming and even now is already in the world. You, dear children, are from God and have overcome them, because the one who is in you is greater than the one who is in the world. They are from the world and therefore speak from the viewpoint of the world, and the world listens to them. We are from God, and whoever knows God listens to us; but whoever is not from God does not listen to us. This is how we recognize the Spirit of truth and the spirit of falsehood.* **1 John 4:1–6**

It is important for believers not to accept unquestioningly everything that is told us by teachers. The "world" here is those who oppose the things of God. False prophets and teachers really belong to the world, so it is not surprising that they are accepted by the world or that those who speak and teach the truth are not accepted. Falsehood may be powerful but truth will prevail. The wickedness around us is frightening. Evil is stronger than us, however, as the Holy Spirit is within us, evil is not stronger than the Holy Spirit.

And so we know and rely on the love God has for us. God is love. Whoever lives in love lives in God, and God in him. In this way love is made complete among us so that we will have confidence on the day of judgment, because in this world we are like him. **1 John 4:16–17**

The Day of Judgment is that time when all people will appear before Christ and be held accountable for their actions. With God living in us through Christ, we have no reason to fear this day, because we have been saved from punishment. Instead, we can look forward to the Day of Judgment, because it will mean the end of sin and the beginning of a face-to-face relationship with Jesus Christ. (*Life Application Bible*, pg. 2282)

Sometimes a guilty root is responsible for the tormenting fear of judgment in a born again person. Although we have asked God's forgiveness, the devil continues to accuse us and make us feel unworthy of forgiveness. Actually, no one is worthy of forgiveness. Forgiveness is ours by the grace of God. As long as a believer permits the devil to condemn them, their peace will be destroyed and they will have no assurance that God will answer their prayers. (Hammond, *Demons and Deliverance*, pg. 47)

———————

They overcame him by the blood of the Lamb and by the word of their testimony; they did not love their lives so much as to shrink from death. Therefore rejoice, you heavens and you who dwell in them! But woe to the earth and the sea, because the devil has gone down to you!
Revelation 12:11–12

The real means of the dragon's overthrow was the atoning work of Christ; His people share that victory by their testimony to His saving power in their lives. The initiation of the kingdom of God through the redemption on the cross, our Lord's death and resurrection were the occasion of Satan's downfall and the establishment of the kingdom age with all its blessings. Satan can no longer fulfill his function of falsely accusing the saints before God; for Christ has secured our acquittal and reconciled us to God through his atonement.

The end times draw nearer daily and scripture tells us Satan will step up the battle. His attacks will be more intense. We can overcome Satan because we are washed free of sin by the blood of the Lamb of God. Christ atoned for our sins on the cross. We can overcome Satan by giving our own testimony. The most powerful words that one can ever speak on behalf of Jesus is our personal testimony. Through our testimonies, we can share what Jesus has meant to us in our lives. This is how we can overcome evil.

———————

> *I warn everyone who hears the words of the prophecy of this book: If anyone adds anything to them, God will add to him the plagues described in this book. And if anyone takes words away from this book of prophecy, God will take away from him his share in the tree of life and in the holy city, which are described in this book.*
> Revelation 22:18–19

This warning is given to those who might purposefully distort the message in this book. We too must handle the Bible with care and great respect so we do not distort its message, even unintentionally. We should be quick to put its principles into practice in our lives. No human explanation or interpretation of God's Word should be elevated to the same authority as the text itself. (*Life Application Bible*, pg. 2334)

If one communicates with evil spirits, he may become convinced that he has gained special information about the devil's hierarchy, the devil's plans, or other revealing knowledge. If a person accepts such information and teaches it as truth, then he has fallen in deception. (Hammond, *Demons and Deliverance*, pg. 24)

Do's And Don'ts

No one becomes an expert in spiritual warfare. Almost every time we face a confrontation against darkness, we will find ourselves completely baffled at what to do next. These are some do's and don'ts which should be emphasized in spiritual warfare.

- Don't allow or accept any information or communication from a spirit. Communication with them is only for the purpose of binding them and commanding them to leave.
- Don't believe anything they say without testing it. The way to do that is by asking: "Will that answer or information stand as truth before the throne of the true and living God?"
- Don't be afraid of their threats of harm. Quote scripture i.e., "He that is begotten of God keepth himself, and that wicked one cannot touch him" (1 John 5:18b). Our protection is the Lord, and they cannot hurt us when our Lord is shielding us.
- Don't assume that one victory is the end of warfare. Remember that whether we are afflicted with deep struggles with darkness or not we need to maintain a close walk with the Lord Jesus Christ.
- Don't rely upon bold confrontation as the only way to victory over the enemy. Daily application of doctrinal, warfare prayer, scripture memorization, and a walk of praise toward God are essential.

- Don't forget to fill the void left by the demons with Godly things, the study of scripture, prayer, fellowship with other believers, etc.
- Don't forget we are only to judge ourselves not others.
- Don't ever underestimate the constant pressure Satan applies to lead us into sin; to separate us from God; to compromise God's Word.
- Don't forget how important intercessory prayer can be.
- Do daily put on the whole armor of God and claim your union with Christ and walk in the fullness of the spirit.
- Do take back all the ground you may have given Satan by careless willful sins of the flesh. Do this through a simple prayer for forgiveness.
- Do bind all powers of darkness working under any wicked spirits to him, commanding them all to leave when he leaves.
- Do force the wicked spirits to admit that because we are seated with Christ far above all principalities and powers (Ephesians 1:21, 2:6) that we have full authority over them.
- Do force them to admit that when you command them to leave that they have to go where Christ sends them.
- Do demand that if the wicked spirit has divided into several parts, that he become a whole spirit.
- Do be prepared for the wicked power to try to hurt you. Evil spirits can interfere by using sudden body pains, headaches, stomachaches, choking and the like. Command the power, name the symptom, to

release his hold and leave immediately in the name of the Lord Jesus Christ (Bubeck, *The Adversary*, pg. 124–125)

- Do remember your strength comes from God, not you.
- Do remember that forgiveness of people, things, or situations that have hurt/harmed you is essential in spiritual warfare.
- Do remember that there is no person so sinful that God would not forgive them.
- Do remember that Satan uses any means, physical, emotional and spiritual to separate us from God.

Cautions

"The Angels of God" Carolyne Rogerson; handout, 1998

- Remember the Holy Spirit dwells within you. *"He who is within you is greater than he who is within the world."* God who is in you is greater than Satan who is in the world. Call on the strength of the Holy Spirit.
- Never pray to Satan.
- Speak directly to Satan. Do it succinctly and directly.
- Do not linger long in the presence of Satan. Say what you need to say and turn immediately back to God.
- Speak out loud. Satan cannot read your mind (Remember, Satan is not the opposite of God.)
- Speak in the name of Jesus.
- Quote scripture to Satan, if possible.

In The Name Of Jesus Christ, we bind Satan through the authority that is the name of Jesus Christ. Jesus overcame Satan when He gave His life on the cross. We, as believers, approach God through Jesus. Jesus said in John 14:6–7, *"I am the way, the truth and the life. No one comes to the Father except through me. If you really knew me, you would know my Father as well. From now on, you do know him and have seen him."*

Several times on the night before Jesus died, He said, *"Ask in my name."* It is through Jesus that we approach God. We often end our prayers with "in the name of Jesus." It is also through Jesus that we have the authority and power to resist Satan. We have no authority on our own. We have no power on our own. It is in the name of Jesus that we bind Satan. There is no other way.

A Sample Rebuke Of Satan And Warfare Prayers To God

In today's world we pray for each other, however; rarely are these prayers' warfare prayers. There have been so few times in my spiritual life that I have used true prayers of war against evil or against the devil. I believe that we are called to intercede through prayer and that this intercession should also include aggressive warfare prayers.

Before we can put on the armor of God, we must first confess and ask forgiveness. Take time to search your heart before God; ask Him to show you your heart. Don't search your own heart with your natural mind; let the Holy Spirit lead you in the search.

If you are like me, I at times have trouble knowing what to say and how to say it. I want to pray, both in private and in public, but fear is a real presence in prayer. The disciples had the same problem, or they would not have found the need to ask Jesus to teach them to pray. I believe we are no different. We need to learn to pray. I found myself learning to pray by reading and praying other people's prayers; those who have already learned HOW to pray. Therefore, I have included prayers to assist you as you learn to pray.

PRAYER OF CONFESSION

Father, I thank you for the blood of Jesus that cleanses me from all my sin. I come before You in the name of Jesus and ask to be restored to a right relationship with You and my brothers and sisters in Christ.

Father, Your Word says that if I confess my sin, You are faithful and just to forgive me and cleanse me from all unrighteousness. I come into Your presence to confess my sin of _____, knowing that I can draw near to You with a true heart in full assurance of faith, having my heart sprinkled from an evil conscience and my body washed with the pure water of Your Word.

Be gracious to me, Father. Blot out my transgression of ____ _____. Wash me thoroughly from this iniquity and cleanse me from my sin. It is only against You, Lord, that I have sinned and done what is evil in Your sight. I ask Your forgiveness.

I now rejoice, not that I was made sorrowful, but that I was made sorrowful to the point of repentance. My repentance, according to Your will, leads me to eternal life with You. I receive Your abundant life where I was dead in sin. For the law of the Spirit of life in Christ Jesus had made me free from the law of sin and death. And whom the Son sets free shall be free indeed. Blotting out the handwriting of ordinances that were against me, which was contrary to me. You took it out of the way by taking it to Your cross. I choose now to walk under this new covenant of liberty in Your Spirit life.

Father, I thank You that You have blotted out my sins, and as far as the east is from the west is how far You have removed them from me. I declare that this day my sin will be remembered no more, and if Satan brings it up again, he will have to deal with You. Amen.

(Alves, *Becoming A Prayer Warrior*, pg. 54)

PRAYER OF FORGIVENESS

Father, I come before Your throne with a heavy heart because _____ has offended me and I have unforgiveness. I know unforgiveness is contrary to Your Word. Because of this, I have been tormented in my mind and emotions. This has created a binding tie between me and _____.

Therefore, I ask, Father, that You forgive my sins of _____ _____, and I also forgive _____ as you have forgiven me. I repent and let go of all bitterness, wrath, anger, clamor, slander, animosity and malice. I receive my forgiveness in Jesus' name and by His precious blood.

Thank You, Father, for setting _____ and me free from all mental and emotional torment. I will not give the devil an opportunity. I will guard my mouth and let no unwholesome word come forth concerning _____. I will speak words of life, power, health and healing. I will not grieve the Holy Spirit. I will be kind, tenderhearted, forgiving other people as You have forgiven me. I will not return evil for evil, or insult for insult, but I will speak words of blessing upon _____.

In Jesus' name, I command freedom to my body, soul, spirit, family and finances, because I am no longer under the curse of the law but have received my liberty.

I ask that the Holy Spirit rule in my life, bearing fruit to please You. Today I put off my old nature and put on Your love, joy, peace, patience, kindness, goodness, faithfulness, gentleness and self-control.

By a choice of my will, I make a fresh commitment to You, Lord, that I will live in peace with the saints and with my friends, coworkers, neighbors and family. Amen. (Alves, *Becoming A Prayer Warrior*, pg. 56)

FOR PUTTING ON THE ARMOR OF GOD EVERY DAY!

Dear Lord and heavenly Father, Humbly I approach the God and Father of our Lord Jesus Christ. I come before you in the merit, the holiness, and the righteousness of the Lord Jesus Christ. Let the Holy Spirit intercede for me and in me during this time of prayer. I enter by faith into the full power and authority of my Lord's resurrection. Lead me into a deeper understanding of the power of the resurrection. I bring the truth of my Lord's victory over the grave against all of Satan's workings against your will and plan for my life. Because of my union with my Savior, I affirm my full authority and position of victory over Satan and his entire kingdom of darkness. Thank you, Lord Jesus for watching over me and leading me, that Satan may gain no advantage over me. Grant me wisdom to discern the entire devil's deceiving and temptations. By faith I invite the Person of the Holy Spirit to bring the fullness of all of His person and my Lord's work into all areas of my being, I ask the Holy Spirit to fill my mind, my will, and my emotions with His control. Bring all parts of my being into wholeness and submission to the Lord Jesus Christ. I give all my body and appetites to the control of the Holy Spirit for transformation. Enable my spirit to be in fellowship with the Father, the Son, and the Holy Spirit throughout this day. It is in the name of the Lord Jesus Christ with thanksgiving that I bring these supplications before you.

Heavenly Father, I bow in worship and praise before You. I cover myself with the blood of the Lord Jesus Christ as my protection during this time of prayer. I surrender myself completely and unreservedly in every area of my life. I take a stand against the workings of Satan that would hinder me in this time of prayer, and I address myself to the true and living God.

Satan, I command you, in the name of the Lord Jesus Christ, to leave my presence with all your demons and I bring the blood of the Lord Jesus Christ between us.

Heavenly Father, come and open my eyes that I might see how great You are and how complete Your provision for this new day. I desire to be obedient by being strong in the Lord and the power of Your might. I see that this is Your will and purpose for me. I recognize that it is essential to put on the armor that You have provided, and I do so now with gratitude and praise that You have provided all I need to stand in victory against Satan and his kingdom. Grant me wisdom to discern the tactics and sneakiness of Satan's strategy against me. Enable me to wrestle in victory against the princes, powers, rulers, and wicked spirits that carry the battle of darkness against me.

I delight to take the armor You have provided and by faith to put it on as effective spiritual protection against the spiritual forces of darkness.

I confidently take the girdle of truth that You offer me. I take Him who is the truth as my strength and protection. I reject Satan's lies and deceiving ways to gain advantage against me. Grant me discernment and wisdom to cause me to see and not accept his lies as truth. I desire to believe only the truth. I worship and praise You that You lead me only in the ways of truth. Thank You that Satan cannot stand against the bold use of truth.

Thank You for the breastplate of righteousness, which you offer me. I eagerly accept it and put it on as my protection.

Thank You for reminding me again that all of my righteousness comes from You. I embrace that righteousness which is mine by faith in the Lord Jesus Christ. It is His righteousness, which is mine by faith in the Lord Jesus Christ. His righteousness is mine through justification. I reject and repudiate all trust in my own righteousness, which are as filthy rags. I ask You to cleanse me of all the times I have counted my own goodness as being acceptable before You. I bring the righteousness of my Lord directly against all of Satan's workings against me. I express my desire to walk in righteousness before God today. By faith I appropriate the righteousness of Christ and invite Him to walk in His holiness in my life today that I might experience His righteousness in total context of ordinary living. I count upon the righteousness of my Lord to be my protection. I know that Satan must retreat from before the righteousness of God.

Thank You, Lord, for the sandals of peace You have provided. I desire that my feet should stand on the solid rock of the peace that You have provided. I claim the peace with God, which is mine through justification. I desire the peace of God, which touches my emotions and feelings through prayer and sanctification. Thank You that as I walk in obedience to You, that as the God of peace You are putting Satan under my feet. I will share this good news of peace with all others today that Your Spirit will bring into my life and witness. Thank You for You have not given me the spirit of fear but of love and power and a sound mind. Thank You that Satan cannot stand against Your peace.

Eagerly, Lord, I lift up the shield of faith against all the blazing missiles that Satan and his hosts' fire at me. I recognize that You are my shield and that in Your incarnation and crucifixion You took the arrows of Satan, which I deserved. By faith I count upon You to shield me from above and beneath; on my right and my left; in front of me and behind me, that I might be protected, walled in, encapsulated by You that Satan may gain no way to hurt or destroy me from fulfilling Your will today. I am willing that any fiery darts of Satan You wish to touch me should do so, but I shall look upon them as refining fires permitted in Your providence for my refining and glory.

Thank You, Lord that You are a complete and perfect shield and that Satan cannot touch me apart from Your sovereign purpose.

I recognize that my mind is a particular target of Satan's deceiving ways. I take from You the helmet of salvation. I cover my mind, my thoughts, with Your salvation. I recognize that the Lord Jesus Christ is my salvation. I helmet my head with Him. I invite His mind to be in me. Let me think His thoughts, feel His love and compassion, and discern His will and leading in all things. Let my mind be occupied with the continuing, daily, saving work of my Lord in and through my life. May the salvation of my Lord meet and defeat all satanic thoughts that come to my mind.

With joy I take hold upon the sword of the Spirit, which is the Word of God. I affirm that Your Word is the trustworthy, infallible Word of God. I choose to believe it and to live in its truth and power. Grant me the love for Your Word, which comes from the Holy Spirit. Forgive and cleanse me from the sin of neglecting Your Word. Enable me to memorize it and to meditate upon its truth. Grant me proficient recall and skill in using Your Word against all of Satan's subtle attacks against me, even as my Lord Jesus Christ used the Word against Satan. Enable me to use Your Word not only to defend me from Satan, but also to claim its promises and to wield the sword strong against Satan to defeat him, to push him back, to take away from him ground he claims, and to win great victories for my God through Your Word. Thank You that Satan must retreat from Your Word applied against him.

Thank you, dear Lord, for prayer. Help me to keep this armor well oiled with prayer. I desire to pray at all times with depth and intensity as the Holy Spirit leads me. I reject all fleshly praying as sin. I trust the Holy Spirit to enable me, to intercede for me and through me. Grant me great supplication and burden for others in God's family of blood-washed saints. Enable me to see their needs and to assist them through prayer as the enemy attacks them. I am thankful, heavenly Father, for the expression of Your will for my daily life as You have shown me in Your Word; I therefore claim all the will of God for today. I am grateful that You have made a provision so that today I can live filled with the Spirit of God with love, joy, and self-control in my life. I recognize that this is Your will for me and I therefore reject and resist all the endeavors of

Satan and of his demons to rob me of the will of God. I claim the fullness of the will of God for today.

I do, in the name of the Lord Jesus Christ, completely surrender myself to You, heavenly Father, as a living sacrifice. I choose no to be conformed to this world. I choose to be transformed by the renewing of my mind, and I pray that You would show me Your will and enable me to walk in all the fullness of Your will for me today. I smash the strongholds of Satan formed against my body, mind and will today, and recognize that I am Your temple; and I rejoice in Your mercy and Your goodness.

Heavenly Father, I pray that now through this day You would quicken me; show me the way that Satan is hindering and tempting and lying and counterfeiting and distorting the truth in my life. Enable me to be the kind of person that would please You. Enable me to be aggressive in prayer. Enable me to be aggressive mentally, to think Your thoughts after You, and to give You Your rightful place in my life. I pray these things in the name of the Lord Jesus Christ with thanksgiving. Amen

All of these petitions, intercessions, and words of praise I offer up before the true and living God in the name and worthy merit of my Lord Jesus Christ. Amen.

FOR OUR DAILY WALK

Blessed heavenly Father, in the name of the Lord Jesus Christ I want to walk in the Spirit today. I ask the Holy Spirit to bring all of the work of the crucifixion and the resurrection of Christ into my life today. I pray that the Holy Spirit produce His fruit within me today. Forgive me, dear Holy Spirit, for all the times that I have grieved or quenched you. Enable me to respond to your grace and be sensitive to your voice. Grant me discernment to avoid being deceived by false spirits. I trust my victory over the flesh today completely into the hands of the Holy Spirit as I let

Him take control of me. In the name of the Lord Jesus Christ, I receive the Holy Spirit into all of my being. Amen. (Bubeck, *The Adversary*, pg. 43).

DAILY WALK

Heavenly Father, I enter by faith today in death with the Lord Jesus Christ on the cross. I appropriate all of the benefit of the crucifixion, which is mine because of my union with Christ. I count myself dead to my old fleshly nature and all of its workings through my union with Christ at the cross. I recognize that my old nature always wants to resurrect itself against You and Your will for my life. However, I will to let it remain dead in death with my Lord on the cross. I am thankful that this absolute truth can be my subjective experience. I recognize that appropriating the death of my flesh is an essential step to victory over these fleshly temptations, which buffet me. Amen. (Bubeck, *The Adversary*, pg. 38)

Dear Heavenly Father, I praise You and honor You as my Lord. You are in control of all things. I thank you that You are always with me and will never leave me nor forsake me. You are the only all-powerful and only wise God. You are the King of Kings and loving in all Your ways. I love You and thank You that I am united with Christ and spiritually alive in Him. I choose not to love the world or the things in the world, and I crucify the flesh and all its passions.

Thank You for the life I now have in Christ. I ask You to fill me with the Holy Spirit so I may say no to sin and yes to You. I declare my total dependence upon You and I take my stand against Satan and all his lying ways. I choose to believe the truth of God's Word despite what my feelings may say, I refuse to be discouraged; You are the God of all hope. Nothing is too difficult for You. I am confident that You will supply all my needs as I seek to live according to Your Word. I thank You that I can be content and live a responsible life through Christ who strengthens me.

I now take my stand against Satan and command him and all his evil spirits to depart from me. I choose to put on the full armor of God so I may be able to stand firm against all the devil's schemes. I submit my body as a living and holy sacrifice to God, and I choose to renew my mind by the living Word of God. By so doing I will be able to prove that the will of God is good, acceptable, and perfect for me. In the name of my Lord and savior, Jesus Christ. Amen. (Anderson, *The Bondage Breaker*, pg. 210)

THE SINNER'S PRAYER

Lord Jesus, I confess that I have sinned against you, and I ask that you forgive me for all my sins. I believe that Jesus Christ is the Son of God, who shed His blood on the cross for the remission of my sins. I give my life to you and ask that you come into my heart that I may live with you eternally, in Jesus name I pray. Amen. (Rogerson, *The Angels of God*, handout)

PRAYER FOR PROTECTION

Lord, I ask you to protect my family _____ (list all of them by name) from sickness, from all harm and from accidents. If any of us has been subjected to any hexes, curses, or spells, I declare these curses, hexes and spells null and void in the name of Jesus Christ. If any evil spirits have been sent against us, I decommission you in the name of Jesus Christ and I send you to Jesus to deal with, as He will. Then, Lord, I ask you to send your holy angels to guard and protect all of us. Amen. (MacNutt, *Deliverance from Evil* Spirits, pg. 279)

REBUKE OF SATAN

Soverign Lord, creator of all good things, thank you for_____

_____ (list by name). Father I pray that you will, through your Holy Spirit draw _____ to yourself. I pray for his/her/their salvation, Lord. I pray that _____ will come to know the Lord Jesus Christ as his/her/their personal Savior.

Now, Satan, I turn to you. I speak to you in the name of Jesus Christ. Through the authority and power of Jesus, I bind and rebuke you on behalf of _____. You cannot have him/her/them. You and all of the evil associated with you must stay away from _____. I especially rebuke _____ (give a personal list of evil for that person . . . materialism, self-sufficiency, illness) and the false security or other effects that it brings. Stay away Satan.

_____ belongs to Jesus. Jesus said, "Let the children come to me." Even though _____ is not a child, he/she is our, or someone's child, and God's child. You cannot stand in the way of that relationship.

And now Lord, I turn to you. Thank you, Father, for loving _ _____. You have proved that you love him/her/them better than we do. What an incredible love that is. Please station your holy angels around _____ and protect him/her/them from hurt and from harm until he/she/they comes to you. In the name of Jesus I pray. Amen. (Rogerson, *The Angels of* God, handout)

INTERCESSORY PRAYER FOR DELIVERANCE FOR YOUR CHILD

(This can also be done for a specific individual, change the words as appropriate)

Loving Father, I bring my child _____ to your throne in prayer. Through the person and work of the Lord Jesus Christ, I present him/her to You as one made perfect and acceptable unto

You. May the blessed Holy Spirit overshadow us during this time of prayer and enable me to pray in the spirit. I bring all powers of darkness seeking to assault _____ and afflict him/her to account before the true and living God. I pray his/her union with the mighty victory of the Lord Jesus Christ directly against them. All powers of darkness seeking to hurt him/her body and soul, I bind up in the name of the Lord Jesus Christ. I loose him/her from their attack and plead over him/her their precious blood of the Lord Jesus Christ. As his/her mother/father and as a priest of God, I claim my place of full authority over all powers of darkness. In your grace, we receive their experience as one having purpose in the sovereign purposes of God. Teach _____and our family through this trial. In the name of the Lord Jesus Christ, Amen.

(This prayer is for when you and your child are together and both are in union with Christ through his blood. If things continue to worsen as you pray, the strength of the spirits present are fighting. Continue with the following prayer)

In the name of the Lord Jesus Christ, I command Satan and all wicked spirits who do not have specific assignment against _____(child's name) to leave his/her presence. I resist you, steadfast in the faith and on the authority of God's Word command you to leave our presence. We do not allow any interference or intrusion into our warfare against the powers of darkness afflicting _____ to be bound aside. You may not work. You may not hurt him/her in any way. There is to be one-way traffic, out of _____ life and to the place where the Lord Jesus Christ sends you. You may never return to afflict _____. I call you to respond through _____faculties. You must answer my questions by giving clear answers through her mind. You may not answer otherwise. I want no talk from you except answers to my questions. I command the chief power of darkness in charge of this affliction of _____, and all related problems to come to attention. I call you to account in the name of the Lord Jesus Christ. What is your name . . . . . . ?

(at this point listen, and continue to command as above as each spirit present, presents themselves to be bound. After you believe that the powers of darkness are fully exposed and bound, proceed to command them to depart as follows)

In the name of the Lord Jesus Christ, I bind you all together; I bind all workers and helpers together. I bind to all hidden replacer or no-name demons that work with him. You may not hurt _____ when you leave him/her presence. I command you to go where the Lord Jesus Christ sends you. I command you to go now. Go to the pit prepared for you in the name of the Lord Jesus Christ.

I now ask the Holy Spirit to come and minister in His fullness and give His peace and joy to _____ life. Amen. (Bubeck, *The Aversary*, pg. 119–122)

INTERCESSORY PRAYER FOR BELIEVERS

Heavenly Father, I bring before You and the Lord Jesus Christ one who is very dear to You and to me, _____. I have come to see that Satan is blinding and binding him/her in awful bondage. He/She is in such a condition that he/she cannot or will not come to You for help on his/her own. I stand in for him/her in intercessory prayer before Your throne. I draw upon the Person of the Holy Spirit that He may guide me to pray in wisdom, power, and understanding.

In the name of the Lord Jesus Christ, I loose _____ from the awful bondage the powers of darkness are putting upon him/her. I bind all powers of darkness set on destroying his/her life. I bind them aside in the name of the Lord Jesus Christ and forbid them to work. I bind up all powers of depression that are seeking to cut _____ off and imprison him/her in a tomb of despondency. I bring in prayer the focus of the Person and work of the Lord Jesus Christ directly upon _____ to his/her strengthening and help. I bring the mighty power of my Lord's incarnation, crucifixion, resurrection, ascension, and glorification directly against all forces of darkness seeking to destroy _____ _____. I ask the Holy Spirit to apply all of the mighty work of the Lord Jesus Christ directly against all forces of darkness seeking to destroy _____.

I pray, heavenly Father, that You may open _____'s eyes of understanding. Remove all blindness and spiritual deafness from his/her heart. As a priest of God in _____'s life, I plead Your mercy over his/her sins of failure and rebellion. I claim all of his/her life united together in obedient love and service to the Lord Jesus Christ. May the Spirit of the living God focus His mighty work upon _____ to grant him/her repentance and to set him/her completely free from all that binds him/her.

In the name of the Lord Jesus Christ, I thank You for Your answer. Grant me the grace to be persistent and faithful in my intercessions for _____, that You may be glorified through this deliverance. Amen. (Bubeck, *The Adversary*, pg. 112–113)

INTERCESSORY PRAYER FOR THOSE THAT DO NOT YET BELIEVE

Loving heavenly Father, in the name of our Lord Jesus Christ, I bring before You in prayer _____. I ask for the Holy Spirit's guidance that I might pray in the Spirit as You have told us. I thank You, heavenly Father, that You have sovereign control over _____. I thank You for the qualities of aggressiveness and leadership, which I see that You have placed in this person. In the name of the Lord Jesus Christ and as a priest of God according to Your Holy Word. I ask for mercy and forgiveness for the sins of _____ by which he/she have grieved

You. I plead the sufficiency of the blood of Christ to meet the full penalty of his/her sins deserve. I claim back the ground of his/her life, which he/she has given to Satan by believing the enemy's deception. In the name of the Lord Jesus Christ, I resist all of Satan's activity to hold _____ in blindness and darkness. Exercising my authority, which is given to me in my union with the Lord Jesus Christ, I pull down the strongholds, which the kingdom of darkness has formed against _____. I smash and break and destroy all those plans formed against _____ mind, will, emotions, and body. I destroy in prayer the spiritual blindness and deafness that Satan keeps upon him/her. I empower to convict, to bring to repentance, and to lead _____ into faith in the Lord Jesus Christ as his/her Savior. I cover him/her with the blood of the Lord Jesus Christ, and I break Satan's power to blind him/her to the truth of God. Believing that Your Holy Spirit is leading me, I claim _____ for You in the name of the Lord Jesus Christ and I thank You for the answer to my prayer. In the name of the Lord Jesus Christ, I joyfully lay this prayer before You in the worthiness of His completed work. Amen. (Bubeck, *The Adversary*, pg. 106)

PRAYER AT BEDTIME

In the name of the Lord Jesus Christ, I submit my mind, and my dream activities only to the work of the Holy Spirit. I bind up all powers of darkness and forbid them to work in my dream abilities or any part of my subconscious while I sleep. Amen. (Bubeck, *The Adversary*, pg. 145)

Thank You, Lord, that You have brought me into Your family and have blessed me with every spiritual blessing in the heavenly places in Christ Jesus. Thank You for this time of renewal and refreshment through sleep. I accept it as one of Your blessings for

Your children, and I trust You to guard my mind and my body during my sleep.

As I have thought about You and Your truth during the day, I choose to let those good thoughts

continue in my mind while I am asleep. I commit myself to You for Your protection against

every attempt of Satan and his demons to attack me during sleep. Guard my mind from

nightmares. I renounce all fear and cast every anxiety upon You, Lord. I commit myself to You

as my rock, my fortress, and my strong tower. May Your peace be upon this place of rest now.

In the strong name of the Lord Jesus Christ, I pray. Amen.

(Anderson, *The Bondage Breaker*, pg. 211)

REJECTING THOUGHTS THAT ARE NOT OF GOD

In the name of the Lord Jesus Christ, I reject this thought and feeling of _____ which is contrary to God's will. I choose to accept only thoughts in harmony with the Holy Spirit, and I cover my thought life with the blood of the Lord Jesus Christ. Amen. (Bubeck, *The Aversary*, pg. 153)

FOR YOUR HOUSEHOLD

Lord; fill this house from top to bottom with your love and grace. May _____and all that dwell here look only to you for help and guidance. Fill them all with your Spirit and deliver them from every kind of evil. Let the blood of Jesus keep them safe forever. In the name of Jesus Christ our Savior. Amen. (Cruz, *Satan on the Loose*, pg. 68)

Heavenly Father, I acknowledge that You are the Lord of heaven and earth. In Your sovereign power and love, You have given me all things to enjoy. Thank You for this place to live. I claim my home as a place of spiritual safety for me and my family, and ask for Your protection from all the attacks of the enemy. As a child of God, raised up and seated with Christ in the heavenly places, I command every evil spirit claiming ground in this place, based on the activities of past or present occupants, including me, to leave and never return. I renounce all curses and spells directed against place. I ask You, heavenly Father, to post Your holy, warring angels around this place to guard it from any and all attempts of the enemy to enter and disturb Your purpose for me and my family. I thank You, Lord, for doing this in the name of the Lord Jesus Christ. Amen. (Anderson, *The Bondage Breaker*, pg. 211)

FOR YOUR CHILDREN

I bow humbly before the heavenly Father to intercede for my child, _____. I bring him/her before You in the name of the Lord Jesus Christ. I thank You that You have loved _____ with the love of Calvary. I thank You that You gave him/her to us to love and nurture in Christ. I ask You to forgive us for all of our failures to guide him/her in the way he/she ought to go. I am thankful that You are sovereign and can use even the depths of sin to which he/she is now enslaved to bring to your glory. I praise You for this great trial that humbles my heart before You. Accepting my position of being "mighty through God to the pulling down of strongholds," I bring all of the work of the Lord Jesus Christ to focus directly against the powers of darkness that blind and bind _____. I pray the victory of our Lord's incarnation, crucifixion, resurrection, ascension, and glorification directly against all of Satan's power in _____'s life. I bind up all powers of darkness set to destroying _____, and I loose him/her from their blinding in the name of the Lord Jesus Christ. I invite the blessed Holy Spirit to move upon _____

heart and to convict him/her of sin, of righteousness and of judgment to come. In my priestly ministry, in confess _____ sins
unto You and plead Your compassionate mercy toward him/her.
I confess his/her yielding to all manner of fleshly sins which has
given Satan such place in his/her life. I plead the blood of Christ
over _____ wickedness and wait upon the Holy Spirit to bring
him/her to repentance, faith, and life in the Lord Jesus Christ. By
faith, I claim him/her for a life yielding to serve the true and living God in the name of the Lord Jesus Christ. Amen. (Bubeck,
The Adversary, pg. 108)

FOR SPOUSES

Loving heavenly Father, I thank You for Your perfect plan for our
marriage. I know that a marriage functioning in Your will and
blessing is fulfilling and beautiful. In the name of the Lord Jesus
Christ, I bring our marriage before You that You might make it all
You desire it to be. Please forgive me for my sins of failure in our
marriage. In the name of the Lord Jesus Christ, I tear down all
of Satan's strongholds designed to destroy our marriage. I break
all relationships between us that have been established by Satan
and his wicked spirits in the name of the Lord Jesus Christ. I will
accept only the relationships established by You and the blessed
Holy Spirit. I invite the Holy Spirit to enable me to relate to ___
_____ in a manner that will meet his/her needs. I submit our
conversation to You, that it may please You. I submit our physical
relationship to You that it may enjoy your blessing. I submit our
love to You that You may cause it to grow and mature. I desire
to know and experience in marriage the fullness of Your perfect
will. Open my eyes to see all areas where I am deceived. Open
_____ eyes to see any of Satan's deception upon him/her.
Make our union to be the Christ-centered and blessed relationship You have designed in Your perfect will. I ask this in the name

of the Lord Jesus Christ with thanksgiving. Amen. (Bubeck, *The Adversary*, pg. 108)

PRAYER OF ANCESTORS

As a child of God purchased by the blood of the Lord Jesus Christ, I here and now renounce and repudiate all the sins of my ancestors. As one who has been delivered from the power of darkness and translated into the kingdom of God's dear Son, I cancel out all demonic working that has been passed on to me and my family from my ancestors. As one who has been crucified with Jesus Christ and raised to walk in newness of life, I cancel every curse that may have been put upon my family and me. I announce to Satan and all his forces that Christ canceled any curses on me for me when He hung on the cross. As one who has been crucified and raised with Christ and now sits with Him in heavenly places, I renounce any and every way in which Satan may claim ownership of my family and me. I declare myself to be eternally and completely signed over and committed to the Lord Jesus Christ. All this I do in the name and authority of the Lord Jesus Christ. (Rockstad, *Booklets and Pamphlets on Spiritual Warfare*, E.B.)

GENERAL PRAYERS

Lord, God, surely You desire truth in my inner parts; You teach me wisdom in the inner most places. Please expose to me the deeply embedded lies I've believed and replace them with permanently engraved truth." Enable me to take the lies as God reveals them to me through prayer and find Scripture to combat that lie. In Jesus'name I pray. Amen

Lord God, You have told us in Your Word that the devil was a murderer from the beginning, not holding to the truth, for there is no truth in him. When he lies, he speaks his native tongue, for he is a liar and the father of lies. Help me to discern that whatever deception exists, the devil is at work. In Jesus' name I pray. Amen

My faithful Father, I desire to become mature, attaining to the whole measure of the fullness of Christ. Then I will no longer be an infant, tossed back and forth by the waves, and blown here and there by every wind of teaching and by the cunning craftiness of men in their deceitful scheming. In Jesus' name I pray. Amen

Father God, You have adamantly warned Your children not to be deceived. Am I presently being deceived in any way? If I am, reveal it to me and give me the courage to cease cooperation with deceptive schemes. In Jesus' name I pray. Amen

I praise You, God of heaven and Lord of earth. You are not a man, that you should lie, nor a son of man, that You should change Your mind. Do You speak and then not act? Do You promise and not fulfill? You are always faithful, God. How grateful I am to know that You will never lie to me. In Jesus' name I pray. Amen

Father God, develop a higher level of discernment in me. Help me to know truth well so that I will quickly recognize the most finely crafted lie. In Jesus' name I pray. Amen

Dear heavenly Father, I acknowledge Your presence in this room and in my life. You are the only omniscient, omnipotent, and omnipresent God. I am dependent upon You, for apart from You I can do nothing. I stand in the truth that all authority in heaven and on earth has been given to the resurrected Christ, and because I am in Christ, I share that authority in order to make disciples and set captives free. I ask You to fill me with Your Holy Spirit and lead me into all truth. I pray for your complete protection and ask for Your guidance. In the name and authority of the Lord Jesus Christ, I command Satan and all evil spirits to release me in order that I can be free to know and to choose to do the will of God. As a Child of God who is seated with Christ in the heavenlies, I command every evil spirit to leave my presence. I belong to God and the evil one cannot touch me. In Jesus name I pray. Amen. (Anderson, *Winning Spiritual Warfare*, pg. 17)

Father, in Jesus' name, I come boldly and with confidence to the throne of grace to obtain mercy and receive grace to help in time of need for _____. Amen. (Alves, *Becoming a Prayer Warrior*, pg. 170)

Father, I ask You to give to _____ Your spirit of wisdom and revelation in the deep, intimate, full knowledge of You, the eyes of their hearts and understanding being enlightened and flooded with light, that they might know what is the hope of their calling, and what are the riches of the glory of Your inheritance in them, and what is the exceeding greatness of Your power toward them, because they do believe according to the working of Your mighty power which You wrought in Christ, when You raised Him from the dead, and set Him at Your own right hand in the heavenly places.

And Father, even as Your servant Moses was faithful in all Your house, and You spoke to him face-to-face, even so I pray that _____ will be faithful and entrusted in all Your house, and that You would speak face-to-face, and mouth-to-mouth with them, openly, clearly, and directly, and not in dark sayings or riddles.

I pray _____ will keep and obey Your commandments and words so that they may continue to abide in Your love, so that You will come unto them and make Your abode and special dwelling place with them, and love them, and show and reveal and manifest Yourself to them, and make Yourself real and be clearly seen by them. Amen. (Alves, *Becoming a Prayer Warrior*, pg. 171)

Father, I ask that the Spirit of the Lord rest upon _____, the spirit of wisdom and understanding, the spirit of counsel and might and strength, the spirit of knowledge and of the reverential and obedient fear of the Lord.

I pray _____ will not be vague or thoughtless or foolish, but will be understanding, firmly grasping the will of the Lord; that they may ever be continually filled with the Holy Spirit, and with the fruit that the Holy Spirit produces; love, joy, peace, patience, kindness, goodness, faithfulness, gentleness and self-control. I pray that _____ walk and live habitually in the Holy Spirit, responsive to, controlled and guided and led by the Holy Spirit, so that they will not gratify or carry out the cravings and desires of the flesh, and not be subject to, or come under the law.

Father, grant that the manifestation of the Spirit be given to _____ to profit them in all they do. That _____ retain the standard of sound words, in the faith and love which are in Christ Jesus, and that You open up to them a door for the Word, so they may speak forth the mystery of Christ, in order that they may make it clear in the way they ought to speak, and that their speech always be with grace, seasoned with salt, so they may know how to response to each person they meet. Amen. (Alves, *Becoming a Prayer Warrior*, pg. 172)

Father, like the Holy One who called them is holy, I pray that _____ may be filled with the knowledge of Your will in all spiritual wisdom and understanding, so that they may walk in a manner worthy of the Lord, to please You in all respects, bearing fruit in every good work and increasing in the knowledge of God, strengthened with all power, according to Your glorious might, for the attaining of all steadfastness and patience.

I pray that You will instruct _____ and teach them in the way they should go, and counsel them with Your eye upon them. Amen. (Alves, *Becoming a Prayer Warrior*, pg. 173)

Father, I pray that _____ will trust in You, in order that loving kindness and mercy may surround them. That they will not trust in people or make flesh their strength, but trust in the Lord that they may be blessed.

I pray _____ will continue in the faith firmly established, grounded and settled, and steadfast, and not be moved away from the hope of the gospel.

I pray they will abide vitally united to You, and that Your words will remain in and continue to live in their hearts, so that _____ may ask whatever they will and it shall be done for them. For You have called and chosen them that they might go and bring forth much fruit, and keep on bearing lasting, remaining, abiding fruit, that You may be honored and glorified, and that _____ may show and prove themselves to be true followers and disciples of Yours.

I pray, Father, that _____ continue building themselves up on their most holy faith, praying in the Holy Spirit, keeping themselves in the love of God, and looking for the mercy of the Lord Jesus Christ unto eternal live.

Now to Him, who is able to establish _____ according to the gospel and the preaching of Jesus Christ, according to the revelation of the mystery which has been kept secret for long ages past, but now is manifested, and by the Scriptures of the prophets, according to the commandment of the eternal God, which has been make known to all the nations, leading to obedience of faith; now to the only wise God, through Jesus Christ, be the glory forever. Amen (Alves, *Becoming a Prayer Warrior*, pg. 174)

Thank You Father, through Jesus Christ for _____; in Jesus' name I bring these requests and petitions before You on their behalf.

Thank You for sending Your Word, the Lord Jesus, and healing _____ and delivering them from their destructions. I give You thanks for Your loving kindness, and for Your wonders to the sons of men. I pray they will also offer You sacrifices of thanksgiving, and tell of Your works with joyful singing.

Father, I pray that _____ give attention to Your words, and incline their ears to Your sayings; that they do not let them depart from their sight, and that they keep them in the midst of their hearts, because they are life to those who find them and health to their whole body.

Thank You, Father, that because _____ serves You, You will bless their bread and their water, and You will remove sickness from their midst.

Father, I pray their souls bless You, and that they not forget any of Your benefits: for You pardon all their iniquities; You heal all their diseases; You redeem their lives from the pit; You crown _____ with loving-kindness and compassion; You satisfy their years and desires with good things so that their youth is renewed like the eagle's; and You, only, perform righteous deeds, and judgments for all who are oppressed.

Father, thank You that the Spirit of Him who raised Jesus from the dead dwells in _____, and that because You raised Jesus from the dead, You will also give life to their mortal bodies through Your Spirit who indwells them.

I thank You, Father, that Jesus, Himself, bore their sins in His own body on the cross, that they might die to sin and live to righteousness; for by His wounds they were healed.

Thank You, Father, that Christ has redeemed _____ from the curse of the Law, having become a curse for them, for it is written, "Cursed is every one who hangs on a tree," in order that in Christ Jesus the blessing of Abraham might come to the Gentiles, that they might receive the promise of the Spirit through faith. Thank You, Father, _____ belong to Christ, and are Abraham's offspring, and heirs according to Your promise. Amen. (Alves, *Becoming a Prayer Warrior*, pg. 189)

Thank You, Father, _____ has been called to freedom; only I pray they do not turn their freedom into an opportunity for the flesh, but through love may they serve one another. For the whole law is fulfilled in one word, in the statement, "You shall love your neighbor as yourself" (Galatians 5:13–14).

I pray, Father, that _____ forgets what lies behind and reach forward to what lies ahead, pressing on toward the goal for the prize of the upward call of God in Christ Jesus. And if in anything they have a different attitude, Father, I pray You reveal it also to them.

So, Father, I pray_____ does nothing from selfishness or empty conceit, but with humility of mind let them regard one another as more important than themselves; that they do not merely look out for their own personal interests, but also for the interests of others. I pray they will have the same attitude in themselves which was also in Christ Jesus. Amen. (Alves, *Becoming a Prayer Warrior*, pg. 190)

Father, I pray that You bless _____, and keep them; that You make Your face to shine on them, and be gracious to them; that You life up Your countenance upon them, and give them peace.

Cause _____ to increase and abound in love for one another, and for all humankind, so that You may establish their hearts unblamable in holiness before You at the coming of our Lord Jesus with all Your saints.

Father, I pray _____ will fear You and keep Your commandments, for this is the whole duty of man and what You require of them for their good; that they fear You; that they walk in all Your ways; that they love You and serve You out of and with their whole hearts, and with all their souls, and with all their minds, their faculties of thought, of quick apprehension, intelligence, keenness of discernment, and moral understanding, and with all their strength. Amen. (Alves, *Becoming a Prayer Warrior*, pg. 191)

O, Father, keep _____ as the apple of Your eye; hide him/her in the shadow of Your wings, from the wicked who despoil him/her, from their deadly enemies, who surround him/her.

Father, contend with those who contend with _____; fight against those who fight against him/her. For their eyes are toward You, O god, the Lord; in You he/she take refuge; do not leave him/her defenseless. Keep him/her from the jaws of the traps which have been set for him/her, and from the snares of those who iniquity. Let the wicked fall into their own nets, while _____ pass by safely. (Alves, *Becoming a Prayer Warrior*, pg. 196)

Father, I ask that You not lead Your servants into temptation, but deliver him/her from evil.

I thank You, Father, that no temptation has overtaken _____ but such as is common to man; for You are faithful, and will not allow him/her to be tempted beyond what he/she are able, but with the temptation, You will provide the way of escape also, that he/she may be able to endure it.

Thank You, Father, that You give greater grace. Therefore, it says, "God is opposed to the proud, but gives grace to the humble." I pray, Father, that _____ submit to You, that he/she may resist the devil and he will flee from them. I pray they will draw near to You, and You will draw near to him/her. I pray that _____ cleanse his/her hands, and purify his/her hearts, in order that he/she will not be double minded.

Father, since Jesus, Himself, was tempted in that which He suffered; He is able to come to the aid of those who are tempted. Since we do not have a High Priest who cannot sympathize with our weaknesses, but one who was tempted in all things as we are, yet without sin, I pray that _____ will therefore draw near with confidence to the throne of grace, that he/she may receive mercy and find grace to help in time of need. Amen. (Alves, *Becoming a Prayer Warrior*, pg. 197)

Father, I pray, that _____ will beware of false prophets, who come to him/her in sheep's clothing, but inwardly are ravenous wolves. I pray _____ will know and recognize them by their fruits. For every good tree bears good fruit, but the rotten trees bears bad fruit.

Father, may _____ see to it that no one misleads him/her, for Jesus said that many will come in His name, saying, "I am the Christ," and will mislead many. For false Christ's and false prophets will arise and will show great signs and wonders, so as to mislead, if possible, even the elect.

Father, I pray _____ will not believe every spirit, but will test the spirits to see whether they are from You, because many false prophets have gone out into the world. By this he/she will know the Spirit of God: every spirit that confesses that Jesus Christ has come in the flesh is from God; and every spirit that does not confess Jesus is not from God; and this is the spirit of the antichrist, of which we have heard that it is coming, and now it is already in the world.

I pray, Father, that _____ not be taken captive through philosophy and empty deception, according to the traditions of men , according to the elementary principles of the world, rather than according to Christ. For in Him he/she has been made complete, and He (Christ) is the overall rule and authority. Amen. (Alves, *Becoming a Prayer Warrior*, pg. 198)

I bless You, Lord, for You daily load _____ with benefits. You are the God of his/her salvation. I bless You, Lord.

Father, Your blessing makes _____ rich, and You add no sorrow with it.

Father, I pray that because _____ are generous, he/she will be blessed.

I pray they be blessed to find wisdom, and gain understanding. For long life is in his/her right hand, and in his/her left hand are riches and honor. He/she is a tree of life to those who take hold of his/her, and happy are _____ who hold him/her fasts.

For You, Lord, give grace and glory; no good thing will You withhold from _____ because he/she walk uprightly. O Lord of hosts, how blessed he/she is because he/she trust in You.

I pray that _____ delight him/her in You, Lord, for You will give him/her the desires of his/her hearts. You know his/her days, and his/her inheritance will be forever. He/she will not be ashamed in the time of evil, and in the days of famine He/she will have abundance. Amen. (Alves, *Becoming a Prayer Warrior*, pg. 204)

Biblical/Spiritual Ways To Grow Toward Victorious Living Through Personal Daily Affirmations

Have you ever thought God is ready to give up on you because instead of walking confidently in faith, you sometimes stumble and fall? Do you ever fear that there is a limit to God's tolerance for your failure? Most Christians can be defeated by that kind of thinking. They believe God is upset with them, that He is ready to dump them or that He has already given up on them because they feel their daily performance is less than perfect.

It is true that the walk of faith can sometimes be interrupted by moments of personal unbelief, rebellion or even satanic deception. During those moments, we think God has surely lost His patience with us and is ready to give up on us. We will probably give up if we think God has given up on us. When this happens, we stop walking by faith in God, slump dejectedly by the side of the road and wonder, what's the use? We feel defeated our purpose for being here is suspended, and Satan is elated.

It has been said that success comes in cans and failure in cant's. Believing you can live a victorious Christian life takes no more effort than believing you can't. So why not believe that you can walk by faith in the power of the Holy Spirit, that you can resist the temptations of the world, the flesh, and the devil, and that you can grow as a Christian. It is your choice.

As Christians why do we live in the negative when we have everything we need to live in the positive? I think it was J. C. Penny who said, "Whether you think you can or whether you think you cannot, either way you will prove yourself right." The Christian community has been somewhat reluctant to buy into the power of positive thinking. But we are called to do more than just think positive; we are called to live through the power of believing the truth.

So how, as Christians, do we think and then live in the positive? Listed below are questions that are taken from God's Word. These questions will expand your knowledge of faith. Building your faith by internalizing these truths will lift you from the miry clay of the cant's. (Anderson. *Victory over the Darkness*, pg. 115–117)

1. Why should I be weak when the Bible says that the Lord is the strength of my life and that I will display strength and take action because I know God (Psalm 27:1; Daniel 11:32)?
2. Why should I be depressed when I have hope and can recall to mind God's loving kindness, compassion and faithfulness (Lamentations 3:21–23)?
3. Why should I feel alone when Jesus said He is with me always and He will never leave me nor forsake me (Matthew 28:20; Hebrews 13:5)?
4. Why should I let the pressures of life bother me when I can take courage knowing that Jesus has overcome the world and its problems (John 16:33)?
5. Why should I feel condemned when the Bible says there is no condemnation for those who are in Christ Jesus (Romans 8:1)?
6. Why should I feel helpless in the presence of others when I know that if God is for me, who can be against me (Romans 8:31)?
7. Why should I feel like a failure when I am more

than a conqueror through Christ who loved me (Romans 8:37)?

8. Why should I lack faith to live for Christ when God has given me a measure of faith (Romans 12:3)?

9. Why should I lack wisdom when I know that Christ became wisdom to me from God and God gives wisdom to me generously when I ask Him for it (I Corinthians 1:30; James 1:5)?

10. Why should I be confused when God is the author of peace and He gives me knowledge through His Spirit who lives in me (1 Corinthians 2:12; 14:33)?

11. Why should I accept defeat when the Bible says that God always leads me in victory (2 Corinthians 2:14)?

12. Why should I ever be in bondage knowing that there is freedom where the Spirit of the Lord is (2 Corinthians 3:17)?

13. Why should I feel worthless when Christ became sin for me so that I might become the righteousness of God (2 Corinthians 5:21)?

14. Why should I feel as if I'm cursed or have bad luck when the Bible says that Christ rescued me from the curse of the law that I might receive His Spirit by faith (Galatians 3:13, 14)?

15. Why should I be unhappy when I, like Paul, can learn to be content whatever the circumstances (Philippians 4:11)?

16. Why should I say I can't, when the Bible says I can do all things through Christ who gives me strength (Philippians 4:13)?

17. Why should I worry about my needs when I know that God will take care of all my needs according

to His riches in glory in Christ Jesus (Philippians 4:19)?

18. Why should I fear when the Bible says God has not given me a spirit of fear, but of power, love and a sound mind (2 Timothy 1:7)?

19. Why should I worry and be upset when I can cast all my anxieties on Christ who cares for me (1 Peter 5:7)?

20. Why should I allow Satan control over my life when He that is in me is greater than he that is in the world (1 John 4:4)?

21. Why do I struggle with pride when I could accomplish nothing except through the leading and power of Christ Jesus (Romans 15:17)?

22. Why do I continue to sin even though I want to do good? It seems that war is being waged between my mind and my body, yet the Bible tells me that there is no condemnation through Christ Jesus. If the Spirit of him who raised Jesus from the dead lives also in you (Romans 7:21–8:11)?

23. Why don't I feel comfortable praying, why can't I seem to find the right words when the Bible promises that the Spirit will help us in our weakness. But that the Spirit himself will intercedes for us with groans that words cannot express (Romans 8:26)?

24. Why do I struggle with sharing my witness when Christ promised that anyone who had faith in Him would do what He had done and would do even greater things than these (John 14:12–14)?

25. Why can't I seem to find peace in my heart when Christ promised the peace of God, which tran-

scends all understanding, will guard your heart and your mind in Christ Jesus (Philippians 4:7)?

You have just finished reading the questions that will expand your faith. But if you are like me, my next question would be . . . okay, I've read this but how do I move to where I believe the scriptures, and how do I act upon it. Just telling me to believe doesn't give me the faith to believe.

All of us have our own history that we fall back on in our thinking and in our actions. In Christ, we are new creations. We therefore have to find ways to become focused in our beliefs. Remove negative thinking and believing. This affirmation is Scriptural and puts Christ firmly in our minds and hearts.

We are involved in a winnable war. Our names are written in the Lamb's Book of Life, and the victory has already been won. Our freedom in Christ, and the freedom of those, to whom we minister, has already been secured. All we need to do is appropriate it and be a good steward of what God has entrusted to us.

In Christ I am accepted

John 1:12	I am God's Child
John 15:15	I am Christ's friend
Romans 5:1	I have been justified
I Corinthians 6:17	I am united with the LORD and one with Him in spirit
I Corinthians 6:20	I am a member of Christ's body
Ephesians 1:1	I am a saint
Ephesians 1:5	I have been adopted as God's child
Ephesians 2:8	I have direct access to God through the Holy Spirit
Colossians 1:14	I have been redeemed and forgiven of all my sins
Colossians 2:10	I am complete in Christ

In Christ, I am secure

Romans 8:1,2	I am free from condemnation
Romans 8:28	I am assured that all things work together for good
Romans 8:31–34	I am free from any condemning charges against me
Romans 8:35–39	I cannot be separated from the love of God
2 Corinthians 1:21,22	I have been established, anointed and sealed by God
Colossians 3:3	I am hidden with Christ in God
Philippians 1:6	I am confident that the good work that God has begun in me will be perfected
Philippians 3:20	I am a citizen of heaven
2 Timothy 1:7	I have not been given a spirit of fear but of power, love, and a sound mind
Hebrews 4:16	I can find grace and mercy in time of need
1 John 5:18	I am born of God and the evil one cannot touch me

In Christ, I am significant

Matthew 5:13	I am the salt and light of the earth
John15:1,5	I am a branch of the true vine, a channel of His life
John 15:16	I have been chosen and appointed to bear fruit
Acts 1:8	I am a personal witness of Christ's
I Corinthians 3:16	I am God's temple
2 Corinthians 5:17–20	I am a minister of reconciliation
2 Corinthians 6:1	I am God's co-worker

Ephesians 2:6	I am seated with Christ in the heavenly realm
Ephesians 2:10	I am God's workmanship
Ephesians 3:12	I may approach God with freedom and confidence
Philippians 4:13	I can do all things through Christ who strengthens me

Neil T. Anderson, *Victory Over Darkness*, pg. 64–65, Regal Books, Ventura, CA 1993.

Statement of Truths

The New Age movement has twisted the concept of faith by saying that we make something true by believing it. No, we can't create reality with our minds; only God can do that. We can only *face* reality with our minds. Faith is choosing to believe and act upon what God says, regardless of feelings or circumstances. Believing something, however, does not make it true. *It is true; therefore, we choose to believe it.*

Just "having faith" is not enough. The key question is whether the object of your faith is trustworthy. If the object of your faith is not reliable, then no amount of believing will change it. That is why our faith must be on the solid rock of God and His Word. That is the only way to live a responsible and fruitful life. On the other hand, if what you believe in is not true, then how you end up living will not be right.

For generations, Christians have known the importance of publicly declaring what they believe. Read aloud the following "Statements of Truth," thinking about what you are saying. You may find it very helpful to read it daily for several weeks to renew your mind with the truth and replace any lies you may believe.

Statement of Truth

1. *I recognize that there is only one true and living God who exists as the Father, Son, and Holy Spirit. He is worthy of all honor, praise, and glory as the One who made all things and holds all things together. (See Exodus 20:2–3; Colossians 1:16–17)*

2. *I recognize that Jesus Christ is the Messiah, the Word who became flesh and dwelt among us. I believe that He came to destroy the works of the devil, and that He disarmed the rulers and authorities and made a public display of them, having triumphed over them. (See John 1:1, 14; Colossians 2:15; I John 3:8)*

3. *I believe that God demonstrated His own love for me in that while I was still a sinner, Christ died for me. I believe that He has delivered me from the domain of darkness and transferred me to His kingdom, and in Him I have redemption, the forgiveness of sins. (See Romans 5:8; Colossians 1:13,14)*

4. *I believe that I am now a child of God and that I am seated with Christ in the heavens. I believe that I was saved by the grace of God through faith, and that it was a gift and not a result of any works on my part. (see Ephesians 2:6,8,9; I John 3:1–3)*

5. *I choose to be strong in the Lord and in the strength of His might. I put no confidence in the flesh, for the weapons of warfare are not of the flesh but are divinely powerful for the destruction of strongholds. I put on the full armor of God. I resolve to stand firm in my faith and resist the evil one. (See 2 Corinthians 10:4; Ephesians 6:10–20; Philippians 3:3)*

6. *I believe that apart from Christ I can do nothing, so I declare my complete dependence on Him. I choose to*

abide in Christ in order to bear much fruit and glorify my Father, I announce to Satan that Jesus is my Lord, I reject any and all counterfeit gifts or works of Satan in my life. (See John 15:1,8)

7. I believe that the truth will set me free and that Jesus is the truth. If He sets me free, I will be free indeed. I recognize that walking in the light is the only path of true fellowship with God and man. Therefore, I stand against all of Satan's deception by taking every thought captive in obedience to Christ. I declare that the Bible is the only authoritative standard for truth and life. (See John 8:32,36; 14:6; 2 Corinthians 10:5; 2 Timothy 3:15–17; I John 1:3–7)

8. I choose to present my body to God as a living and holy sacrifice and the members of my body as instruments of righteousness. I choose to renew my mind by the living Word of God in order that I may prove that the will of God is good, acceptable, and perfect. I put off the old self with its evil practices and put on the new self. I declare myself to be a new creation in Christ. (See Romans 6:13; 12:1,2)

9. By faith, I choose to be filled with the Spirit so that I can be guided into all truth. I choose to walk by the Spirit so that I will not carry out the desires of the flesh. (See John 16:13; Galatians 5:16; Ephesians 5:18)

10. I renounce all selfish goals and choose the ultimate goal of love. I choose to obey the two greatest commandments, to love the Lord my God with all my heart, soul, mind, and strength and to love my neighbor as myself. (See Matthew 22:37–39; I Timothy 1:5)

11. I believe that the Lord Jesus has all authority in heaven and on earth, and He is the head over all rule and

> *authority. I am complete in Him. I believe that Satan*
> *and his demons are subject to me in Christ since I am a*
> *member of Christ's body. Therefore, I obey the command*
> *to submit to God and to resist the devil, and I command*
> *Satan in the name of Jesus Christ to leave my presence.*
> *(See Matthew 28:18; Ephesians 1:19–23; Colossians*
> *2:10; James 4:7)*

Neil T. Anderson, *The Bondage Breaker*, pg. 93–95, Harvest House Publishers, Eugene, OR, 2000

In Closing

True freedom will bloom in our life when we put on the truth of WHO God says we are. Knowing who God wants us to be is not the same as practicing who He wants us to be. When life gets complicated and failure abounds, we must turn our hearts back to the basics. Remember who you are in Christ, practice being who God says you are, and in time, you will be walking in the freedom of Christ.

Also, as for the attacks in your life . . . remember, the more we work for Christ the more we move from being of "interest" to Satan, to being a "concern" to Satan, and from there to being a "threat" to Satan. Remember we become major threats to Satan when we begin to walk relentlessly for and in Christ.

Satan knows from our past that our hearts were and in some cases still are deeply wounded. Remember, Satan asked to "sift" believers. But God can and will use the effects of that sifting for His glory and His good.

Being a Christian isn't simple and effortless for anyone. Those genuinely committed to Christ face a constant struggle and for those who were once involved in the occult, the struggle is magnified many times.

Once I lived in peace, because the devil was sure I was his. Now that I have come out of the darkness into the light, he is like an angry lion. His demons are always around me, but so are Christ's angels, and Christ is stronger than all the demons.

Whenever you preach or teach, KNOW that there are two others beside you. One is Christ. Feel His presence leading and guiding you. But also know that Satan or one of his demons is there too. Know he tries his best to keep people from coming in the first place as well as his attempts to keep people from listening, to distract their thoughts, to prevent them from making a decision for Christ. Know that disruptions are his attempt to draw a veil over the ears of those listening and learning.

Even having salvation through Christ, you may still be attacked by demonic influences trying to regain control of your mind, hours, days, or even weeks later. But you don't have to let them. As you continue to walk in humble submission to God, you can resist the devil and he will flee from you (James 4:7).

The devil is attracted to sin like flies are attracted to garbage. Get rid of the garbage and the flies will depart for smellier places. In the same way, walk in the truth, confessing all sin and forgiving those who hurt you, and the devil will have no place in your life to set up shop.

What a beautiful picture of gaining and keeping your victory in Christ! We call upon Jesus, the ultimate authority and He escorts the enemy of our souls out of our lives.

You have won a very important battle in the ongoing war. The victory can continue to be yours as long as you keep choosing the truth and standing firm in the strength of the Lord. If you become aware of lies you have believed, renounce them and choose the truth. If new, painful memories surface, forgive those who hurt you. If the Lord shows you other areas of sin in your life, confess those promptly.

Continue to walk in the truth that your identity and sense of worth comes through who you are in Christ. Renew your mind with the truth that your *acceptance, security, and significance* are in Christ alone. (Anderson, *The Bondage Breaker*, pg. 233)

Chronological Listing of Scripture

BIBLIOGRAPHY

Alves, Elizabeth, Becoming A Prayer Warrior, Regal Books, Ventura, CA, 1998

Anderson, Neil T, Living Free in Christ, Regal Books, Ventura, CA, 1993

Anderson, Neil T, Victory over the Darkness, Regal Books, Ventura, CA, 2000

Anderson, Neil T., The Bondage Breaker, Harvest House Publishers, Eugene, OR, 2000

Anderson, Neil T., Winning Spiritual Warfare, Harvest House Publishers, Eugene, OR 1990

Baskin, Wade, Dictionary of Satanism, The Citadel Press, Secaucus, NJ, 1972

Braaten, Carl, E. and Jensen, Robert W. Sin, Death, and the Devil, William B. Eerdmans

Publishing Co, Grand Rapids, MI 2000

Brooks, Thomas, Precious Remedies Against Satan's Devices, Banner of Truth, Carlissle, PA, 1984

Brown, Rebecca, Unbroken Curses, Whitaker House, New Kensington, PA, 1995

Bubeck, Mark I; The Adversary; Moody Press, Chicago, IL, 1975.

Cruz, Nicky; Satan on the Loose, Fleming H Revel Co, Old Tappam, NJ, 1973

The Catechism of the Catholic Church, Part One p 98, no 268

Day, Peggy L, An Adversary in Heaven, Scholars Press, Atlanta, GA, 1988

Dickason, C. Fred, Demon Possession and The Christian; Moody Press, Chicago, IL 1987

Davidson, Gustav, A Dictionary of Angels, The Free Press, New York, NY, 1971

Geschiere, Peter, A Modernity of Witchcraft, Univ. Press of Virginia, Charlottesville, VA, 1997

Hammond, Frank, Demons and Deliverance, Impact Christian Books, Kirkwood, MO, 2003

Terry C. Hulbert, Spiritual Warfare, (Paper presented at the annual meeting of The Evangelical Alliance Mission) May 1992

Jeremiah, David, Angels The Host of Heaven, Walk Thru The Bible Ministries, Atlanta, GA 1995

Kelly, Henry Ansgar, The Devil at Baptism, Cornell University Press, Ithica, NY 1985

Konya, Alex, Demons: A Biblically Based Persepctive, Schaumburg, Ill.: Regular Baptist, 1990

Knopf, Alfred, The Life of the Devil, London, 1929

Life Application Bible, New International Version, Tyndal House Publ., Inc, Wheaton, IL 1988

Lightner, Robert, Angels, Satan, and Demons, Thomas Nelson Publishers, Nashville, TN 1998

Ling, Trevor, The Signigicance of Satan, London, England, 1961

Luther, Martin, Table Talk, IV, 5097, cited by Father Louis Coulange, (psed. Joseph Turmell),
London, 1929

Mack, Carol K., Dinah, A Field Guide to Demons, Henry Holt & Co., New York, NY, 1998

MacNutt, Francis, Deliverance from Evil Spirits, Grand Rapids, MI: Chosen Books 1995, p 279

Moore, Beth, Praying God's Word, Broadman & Holman Pub., Nashville, TTN 2000.

Oakes, Edward, Original Sin: A disputation, First Things 87, 1998, pg 16

Peen-Lewis, Jessie, War on the Saints, 9th ed. Thomas E, Lowe, Ltd, 1973

Prince, Derek, They Shall Expell Demons, Chosen Books, Grand Rapids, Michigan, 1998

Renner, Rick; Seducing Spirits and Doctrines of Demons, Rick Renner Ministries, 1988

Robbins, Rossell, The Encyclopedia of Witchcraft and Demonology, Bonanza Books, New   New York, NY, 1959

Rockstad, E.B. Booklets and Pamphlets on Spiritual Warfare. Andover, KS.: Rockstad, 67022.

Rogerson, Carolyne, The Angels of God: A Bible Study, Georgetown, SC, unpublished, 1998

Scanlan, Michael, T.O.R., and Cirner, Randall J. (citation) , Deliverance from Evil Spirits, Servant Books, Ann Arbor, MI 1980

Standard Lesson Commentary, 2002–2003

Tozer, A.W., Born After Midnight, Harrisburg, Christian Publishing, 1959, p43

Turner, Alice K., The History of Hell, Harvest Book, San Diego, CA., 1993

Unger, Merrill F, What Demons can do to Saints, Moody Press, Chicago, Il, 1977

Unger, Merrill F, Demons in the World Today, Wheaton, Il.: Tyndale, 1971

Warner, Timothy, Spiritual Warfare, Crossway Books, Wheaton, IL, 1991

Zeller, George, The Fall of Satan, When Did This Take Place?, Middletown Bible Church, Middletown Conn., n.d., photocopy.

Bio

Rev. Hatchell was born in Kansas and grew up in the tri state region of Kansas, Oklahoma and Arkansas. She currently resides in South Carolina. She has a Masters of Divinity and a Ph.D. in Philosophy concentrating on Biblical Studies. She loves animals, and the outdoors. She likes to canvas and crochet. She has three daughters and one grand-daughter. She has been a parish pastor for 11 years.